PRESENTED TO

BY

DATE

GOD'S WORD FOR YOUR

SENIOR YEAR

BIBLICAL PROMISES TO GUIDE AND PREPARE YOU FOR GRADUATION

HONOR HB BOOKS

Inspiration and Motivation for the Seasons of Life

COOK COMMUNICATIONS MINISTRIES
Colorado Springs, Colorado • Paris, Ontario
KINGSWAY COMMUNICATIONS LTD
Eastbourne, England

Honor Books® is an imprint of
Cook Communications Ministries, Colorado Springs, CO 80918
Cook Communications, Paris, Ontario
Kingsway Communications Ltd., Eastbourne, England

GOD'S WORD FOR YOUR SENIOR YEAR: BIBLICAL PROMISES TO
GUIDE AND PREPARE YOU FOR GRADUATION
Copyright © 2007 HONOR BOOKS

All Scripture quotations, unless otherwise noted, are taken from the *Holy Bible,
New International Version*®. *NIV*®. Copyright © 1973, 1978, 1984 by
International Bible Society. Used by permission of Zondervan. All rights reserved.
Scripture quotations marked CEV are taken from the *Contemporary English Version*
© 1995 by American Bible Society. Used by permission; KJV are taken from the
King James Version of the Bible. (Public Domain); MSG are taken from *THE
MESSAGE*. Copyright © by Eugene H. Peterson 1993, 1994, 1995, 1996, 2000,
2001, 2002. Used by permission of NavPress Publishing Group; NCV are taken
from the New Century Version. Copyright © 1987, 1988, 1991 by Word
Publishing, a division of Thomas Nelson, Inc. Used by permission. All rights
reserved; NIRV are taken from the HOLY BIBLE, NEW INTERNATIONAL
READER'S VERSION®. Copyright © 1996, 1998 International Bible Society.
All rights reserved throughout the world. Used by permission of International
Bible Society; NLT are taken from the *Holy Bible, New Living Translation*, copy-
right © 1996. Used by permission of Tyndale House Publishers, Inc., Wheaton,
Illinois 60189. All rights reserved; NRSV are taken from the *New Revised Standard
Version Bible*, copyright © 1989, Division of Christian Education of the National
Council of the Churches of Christ in the United States of America. Used by permission. All rights reserved; AB are taken from *The Amplified Bible*. Copyright ©
1954, 1987 by The Lockman Foundation. Used by permission; TLB are taken
from *The Living Bible,* © 1971, Tyndale House Publishers, Wheaton, IL 60189;
and WEB are taken from the World English Bible. (Public Domain.)

First printing, 2007
Printed in Canada

1 2 3 4 5 6 7

Cover Design: The DesignWorks Group, Inc., Charles Brock
Interior Design: The DesignWorks Group, Inc.
ISBN 978-1-56292-950-3

CONTENTS

A STUDENT RELIES ON GOD REGARDING ...   129

Introduction

What if all the great promises of God had your name written right on them? Well, they do! God meant every God-breathed word to be his personal message to you. Here are some practical tools for your spiritual journey—precious promises that seniors need most, arranged under convenient topics. Experience each scripture as a message straight from God's lips to your heart.

We pray that as you bring the Scripture into your daily life, God will empower you to experience the success and fulfill the dreams that God has destined for you. Discover a renewed sense of God's loving commitment to you, his child. God bless you as you discover the protection and the power of God's promises to you!

How to Use My Personal Promise Bible

Jesus said, "The words that I speak to you are spirit, and they are life" (John 6:63 NKJV). One of the most effective ways to experience a miraculous change in your life—the kind of change that will propel you toward an exciting future—is to allow God's words to sink deep into your heart through meditation, scripture, and prayer. How?

Take a verse and memorize it. God's truth in you can then open your eyes to his great love for you. To get that truth to an even deeper, life-changing level, take that verse and think on it all day. Ask yourself, "How does this truth affect my life today?"

Next, make these promises personal. Allow God's truth to become his truth to you, and you begin to experience lasting change in your life.

The final step is to pray the words of God back to God. God's promises are his personal assurances to you. Not only will you be transformed by him, but you will become a spiritual encouragement in the lives of those around you.

A CHRISTLIKE HEART
REFLECTS GOD'S . . .

CHARACTER IN A SAINT MEANS THE DISPOSITION
OF JESUS CHRIST PERSISTENTLY MANIFESTED.

—OSWALD CHAMBERS

WE CHRISTIANS HAVE NO VEIL OVER OUR FACES; WE CAN BE
MIRRORS THAT BRIGHTLY REFLECT THE GLORY OF THE LORD.
AND AS THE SPIRIT OF THE LORD WORKS WITHIN US,
WE BECOME MORE AND MORE LIKE HIM.

—2 CORINTHIANS 3:18 TLB

ACHIEVEMENT

Without consultation, plans are frustrated, but with many counselors they succeed.

PROVERBS 15:22 NASB

Form your purpose by asking for counsel, then carry it out using all the help you can get.

PROVERBS 20:18 MSG

The master answered, "You did well. You are a good and loyal servant. Because you were loyal with small things, I will let you care for much greater things. Come and share my joy with me."

MATTHEW 25:21 NCV

Whatever your hand finds to do, do it with your might; for there is no work or device or knowledge or wisdom in the grave where you are going.

ECCLESIASTES 9:10 NKJV

Brothers, I do not consider myself yet to have taken hold of it. But one thing I do: Forgetting what is behind and straining toward what is ahead, I press on toward the goal to win the prize for which God has called me heavenward in Christ Jesus.

PHILIPPIANS 3:13–14

ACHIEVEMENT

"The rain and snow come down from the heavens and stay on the ground to water the earth. They cause the grain to grow, producing seed for the farmer and bread for the hungry. It is the same with my word. I send it out, and it always produces fruit. It will accomplish all I want it to, and it will prosper everywhere I send it."

ISAIAH 55:10–11 NLT

It takes wisdom to have a good family, and it takes understanding to make it strong. It takes knowledge to fill a home with rare and beautiful treasures.

PROVERBS 24:3–4 NCV

Many are the plans in a man's heart, but it is the LORD's purpose that prevails.

PROVERBS 19:21 NRSV

Do you see those who are skillful in their work? They will serve kings; they will not serve common people.

PROVERBS 22:29 NRSV

The Lord by skillful and godly Wisdom has founded the earth; by understanding He has established the heavens.

PROVERBS 3:19 AB

15

ACHIEVEMENT

You did not choose me. I chose you and sent you out to produce fruit, the kind of fruit that will last. Then my Father will give you whatever you ask for in my name.

JOHN 15:16 CEV

"Yes, I am the vine; you are the branches. Those who remain in me, and I in them, will produce much fruit. For apart from me you can do nothing."

JOHN 15:5 NLT

If God doesn't build the house, the builders only build shacks. If God doesn't guard the city, the night watchman might as well nap.

PSALM 127:1 MSG

Four steps to achievement: Plan purposefully, prepare prayerfully, proceed positively, pursue persistently.
—WILLIAM ARTHUR WARD

A CHRISTLIKE HEART REFLECTS GOD'S . . .
COMMITMENT

But the Lord's love for those who respect him continues forever and ever, and his goodness continues to their grandchildren and to those who keep his agreement and who remember to obey his orders.

PSALM 103:17–18 NCV

Blessed are those who keep His testimonies, who seek Him with the whole heart!

PSALM 119:2 NKJV

My eyes will be on the faithful in the land, that they may dwell with me; he whose walk is blameless will minister to me.

PSALM 101:6

The precepts of the LORD are right, giving joy to the heart. The commands of the LORD are radiant, giving light to the eyes.... By them is your servant warned; in keeping them there is great reward.

PSALM 19:8, 11

Commit everything you do to the LORD. Trust him, and he will help you.

PSALM 37:5 NLT

COMMITMENT

They hate worthless people, but show respect for all who worship the LORD. And they keep their promises, no matter what the cost.... Those who do these things will always stand firm.

PSALM 15:4–5 CEV

Love the LORD, all you who belong to him. The LORD protects those who truly believe, but he punishes the proud as much as they have sinned.

PSALM 31:23 NCV

Wait for and expect the Lord and keep and heed His way, and He will exalt you to inherit the land; [in the end] when the wicked are cut off, you shall see it.

PSALM 37:34 AB

All the paths of the LORD are mercy and truth, to such as keep His covenant and His testimonies.

PSALM 25:10 NKJV

O LORD, you will keep us safe and protect us from such people forever.

PSALM 12:7

COMMITMENT

"I am with you always, to the close of the age."

MATTHEW 28:20 RSV

Keep me still established both in a constant assurance,
that you will speak to me at the beginning of every
such [soul] sickness, at the approach of every such sin;
and that, if I take knowledge of that voice then, and
fly to You, You will preserve me from falling, or raise
me again, when by natural infirmities I'm fallen.

—JOHN DONNE

A CHRISTLIKE HEART REFLECTS GOD'S . . .
COMPASSION

He will again have compassion on us. He will tread our iniquities under foot; and you will cast all their sins into the depths of the sea.

MICAH 7:19 WEB

He has made His wonders to be remembered; The LORD is gracious and compassionate.

PSALM 111:4 NASB

Because your heart was responsive and you humbled yourself before the LORD ... I have heard you, declares the LORD.

2 KINGS 22:19

When darkness overtakes the godly, light will come bursting in. They are generous, compassionate, and righteous.

PSALM 112:4 NLT

But this I call to mind, and therefore I have hope: The steadfast love of the LORD never ceases, his mercies never come to an end.

LAMENTATIONS 3:21–22 RSV

COMPASSION

Can a woman forget her nursing child, or show no compassion for the child of her womb? Even these may forget, yet I will not forget you. See, I have inscribed you on the palms of my hands; your walls are continually before me.

ISAIAH 49:15–16 NRSV

What a gift life is to those who stay the course! You've heard, of course, of Job's staying power, and you know how God brought it all together for him at the end. That's because God cares, cares right down to the last detail.

JAMES 5:11 MSG

But you, Lord, are a merciful and gracious God, slow to anger, and abundant in lovingkindness and truth.

PSALM 86:15 WEB

Anyone who is kind to poor people lends to the Lord. God will reward him for what he has done.

PROVERBS 19:17 NIRV

COMPASSION

Then you and your children will return to the LORD your God, and you will obey him with your whole being in everything I am commanding you today. Then the LORD your God will give you back your freedom. He will feel sorry for you, and he will bring you back again from the nations where he scattered you.

DEUTERONOMY 30:2–3 NCV

Jesus also said to the man who had invited Him, "When you give a dinner or a supper, do not invite your friends or your brothers or your relatives or your wealthy neighbors, lest perhaps they also invite you in return, and so you are paid back. But when you give a banquet or a reception, invite the poor, the disabled, the lame, and the blind. Then you will be blessed (happy, fortunate, and to be envied), because they have no way of repaying you, and you will be recompensed at the resurrection of the just (upright)."

LUKE 14:12–14 AB

COMPASSION

"For if you return to the LORD, your brothers and your sons will find compassion before those who led them captive and will return to this land. For the LORD your God is gracious and compassionate, and will not turn His face away from you if you return to Him."

2 CHRONICLES 30:9 NASB

God is always fair. He will remember how you helped his people in the past and how you are still helping them. You belong to God, and he won't forget the love you have shown his people.

HEBREWS 6:10 CEV

The mercies of God work compassion to others. A Christian is a temporal savior. They feed the hungry, clothe the naked, and visit the widow and orphan in their distress; among them they sow the golden seeds of charity.

—THOMAS WATSON

CONFIDENCE

It [the gospel] is also the cause of all this trouble I'm in. But I have no regrets. I couldn't be more sure of my ground—the One I've trusted in can take care of what he's trusted me to do right to the end.

2 TIMOTHY 1:12 MSG

So do not lose the courage you had in the past, which has a great reward.

HEBREWS 10:35 NCV

Among the gods there is none like You, O Lord; Nor are there any works like Your works. For You are great, and do wondrous things; You alone are God. For great is Your mercy toward me, and You have delivered my soul from the depths of [Hell].

PSALM 86:8, 10, 13 NKJV

Who is God except the Lord? Who is the Rock except our God? God gives me strength for the battle. He makes my way perfect.

2 SAMUEL 22:32–33 NIRV

CONFIDENCE

◆

For the LORD will be your confidence and will keep your foot from being snared.

PROVERBS 3:26

If you believe, you will receive whatever you ask for in prayer.

MATTHEW 21:22 NLT

Christ is faithful as a son over God's house. And we are his house, if we hold on to our courage and the hope of which we boast.

HEBREWS 3:6 WEB

A wise man suspects danger and cautiously avoids evil, but the fool bears himself insolently and is [presumptuously] confident.

PROVERBS 14:16 AB

And the effect of righteousness will be peace, and the result of righteousness, quietness and trust for ever.

ISAIAH 32:17 RSV

"[God] has fixed a day on which he will have the world judged in righteousness by a man whom he has appointed, and of this he has given assurance to all by raising him from the dead."

ACTS 17:31 NRSV

25

CONFIDENCE

For when we brought you the Good News, it was not only with words but also with power, for the Holy Spirit gave you full assurance that what we said was true. And you know that the way we lived among you was further proof of the truth of our message.

I THESSALONIANS 1:5 NLT

We also have a great priest over the house of God. So let us come near to God with an honest and true heart. Let us come near with a faith that is sure and strong. Our hearts have been sprinkled. Our minds have been cleansed from a sense of guilt. Our bodies have been washed with pure water.

HEBREWS 10:21–22 NIRV

Let us, then, feel very sure that we can come before God's throne where there is grace. There we can receive mercy and grace to help us when we need it.

HEBREWS 4:16 NCV

"If you make yourselves at home with me and my words are at home in you, you can be sure that whatever you ask will be listened to and acted upon."

JOHN 15:7 MSG

CONFIDENCE

Thanks be to God, who always leads us in victory through Christ. God uses us to spread his knowledge everywhere like a sweet-smelling perfume.

2 CORINTHIANS 2:14 NCV

Being confident of this very thing, that he who began a good work in you will complete it until the day of Jesus Christ.

PHILIPPIANS 1:6 WEB

Such is the reliance and confidence that we have through Christ toward and with reference to God. Not that we are fit (qualified and sufficient in ability) of ourselves to form personal judgments or to claim or count anything as coming from us, but our power and ability and sufficiency are from God. [It is He] Who has qualified us [making us to be fit and worthy and sufficient] as ministers and dispensers of a new covenant [of salvation through Christ], not [ministers] of the letter (of legally written code) but of the Spirit; for the code [of the Law] kills, but the [Holy] Spirit makes alive.

2 CORINTHIANS 3:4–6 AB

Jesus Christ is the same yesterday, today, and forever.

HEBREWS 13:8 NKJV

27

CONFIDENCE

[Abraham was] sure that God would make good on what he had said.

ROMANS 4:21 MSG

God wants us to be victors, not victims; to grow, not grovel; to soar, not shrink; to overcome, not to be overwhelmed.
—WILLIAM ARTHUR WARD

28

A CHRISTLIKE HEART REFLECTS GOD'S . . .
COURAGE

You will know that God's power is very great for us who believe. That power is the same as the great strength God used to raise Christ from the dead and put him at his right side in the heavenly world.

EPHESIANS 1:19–20 NCV

Praise the LORD! How blessed is the man who fears the LORD, who greatly delights in His commandments. His descendants will be mighty on earth; the generation of the upright will be blessed.

PSALM 112:1–2 NASB

Take courage as you fulfill your duties, and may the LORD be with those who do what is right.

2 CHRONICLES 19:11 NLT

For the weapons of our warfare are not carnal but mighty in God for pulling down strongholds, casting down arguments and every high thing that exalts itself against the knowledge of God, bringing every thought into captivity to the obedience of Christ.

2 CORINTHIANS 10:4–5 NKJV

COURAGE

Light rises in the darkness for the upright; the LORD is gracious, merciful, and righteous.... He is not afraid of evil tidings; his heart is firm, trusting in the LORD.

PSALM 112:4, 7 RSV

"These things I have spoken to you, that in Me you may have peace. In the world you will have tribulation; but be of good cheer, I have overcome the world."

JOHN 16:33 NKJV

God didn't give us a spirit that makes us weak and fearful. He gave us a spirit that gives us power and love. It helps us control ourselves.

2 TIMOTHY 1:7 NIRV

Wait for the LORD; be strong and take heart and wait for the LORD.

PSALM 27:14

Only be strong and very courageous, to observe to do according to all the law, which Moses my servant commanded you: don't turn from it to the right hand or to the left, that you may have good success wherever you go.

JOSHUA 1:7 WEB

COURAGE

You will give us victory and crush our enemies.

PSALM 60:12 CEV

[God Almighty] will cover you with his pinions, and under his wings you will find refuge; his faithfulness is a shield and buckler. You will not fear the terror of the night, nor the arrow that flies by day, nor the pestilence that stalks in darkness, nor the destruction that wastes at noonday.

PSALM 91:4–6 RSV

God's now at my side and I'm not afraid; who would dare lay a hand on me? God's my strong champion; I flick off my enemies like flies.

PSALM 118:6–7 MSG

The LORD helps them and delivers them; he delivers them from the wicked and saves them, because they take refuge in him.

PSALM 37:40

Be strong, courageous, and firm; fear not nor be in terror before them, for it is the Lord your God Who goes with you; He will not fail you or forsake you.

DEUTERONOMY 31:6 AB

COURAGE

My defense is of God, Who saves the upright in heart.

PSALM 7:10 NKJV

Far better it is to dare mighty things, to win glorious triumphs, even though checkered by failure, than to take rank with those poor spirits who neither enjoy much nor suffer much because they live in the gray twilight that knows not victory nor defeat.

—THEODORE ROOSEVELT

A CHRISTLIKE HEART REFLECTS GOD'S . . .
EMPOWERMENT

◆

God has spoken once, twice I have heard this: That power belongs to God.

PSALM 62:11 NKJV

I will sing of your strength. Yes, I will sing aloud of your lovingkindness in the morning. For you have been my high tower, a refuge in the day of my distress.

PSALM 59:16 WEB

God chose what is foolish in the world to shame the wise, God chose what is weak in the world to shame the strong.

I CORINTHIANS 1:27 RSV

God is awesome in his sanctuary. The God of Israel gives power and strength to his people. Praise be to God!

PSALM 68:35 NLT

Who rules by his might forever, whose eyes keep watch on the nations—let the rebellious not exalt themselves.

PSALM 66:7 NRSV

The Almighty is beyond our reach and exalted in power; in his justice and great righteousness, he does not oppress.

JOB 37:23

EMPOWERMENT

The kingdom of God is not a matter of talk. It is a matter of power.

I CORINTHIANS 4:20 NIRV

Our Lord is great and very powerful. There is no limit to what he knows.

PSALM 147:5 NCV

He energizes those who get tired, gives fresh strength to dropouts.

ISAIAH 40:29 MSG

We preach Christ crucified, to Jews a stumbling block and to Gentiles foolishness, but to those who are the called, both Jews and Greeks, Christ the power of God and the wisdom of God.

I CORINTHIANS 1:23–24 NASB

The message about the cross doesn't make any sense to lost people. But for those of us who are being saved, it is God's power at work.

I CORINTHIANS 1:18 CEV

EMPOWERMENT

We possess this precious treasure [the divine Light of the Gospel] in [frail, human] vessels of earth, that the grandeur and exceeding greatness of the power may be shown to be from God and not from ourselves.

2 CORINTHIANS 4:7 AB

Our Almighty Parent delights to conduct the tender nestlings of His care to the very edge of the precipice, and even to thrust them off into the steeps of air that they may learn their possession of unrealized power of flight, to be forever a luxury. And if, in the attempt, they be exposed to unwanted peril, He is prepared to swoop beneath them, and to bear them upward on His mighty pinions.

—LETTIE B. COWMAN

ENCOURAGEMENT

A generous man will prosper; he who refreshes others will himself be refreshed.

PROVERBS 11:25

Kind words are like honey—sweet to the soul and healthy for the body.

PROVERBS 16:24 NLT

Hear, for I will speak noble things, and from my lips will come what is right; for my mouth will utter truth; wickedness is an abomination to my lips.

PROVERBS 8:6–7 RSV

I am poor and needy; hasten to me, O God! You are my Help and my Deliverer; O Lord, do not tarry!

PSALM 70:5 AB

I will remember [God's] deeds; for I will remember your wonders of old. I will also meditate on all your work, and consider your doings.... You are the God who does wonders. You have made your strength known among the peoples.

PSALM 77:11–12, 14 WEB

ENCOURAGEMENT

The Lord GOD has given Me the tongue of disciples, that I may know how to sustain the weary one with a word. He awakens Me morning by morning, He awakens My ear to listen as a disciple.

ISAIAH 50:4 NASB

The LORD is close to everyone who prays to him, to all who truly pray to him. He gives those who respect him what they want. He listens when they cry, and he saves them.

PSALM 145:18–19 NCV

Don't laugh when we suffer, you enemies of ours! We have fallen. But we'll get up. Even though we sit in the dark, the Lord will give us light.

MICAH 7:8 NIRV

Timely advice is as lovely as golden apples in a silver basket.

PROVERBS 25:11 NLT

He will regard the prayer of the destitute, and will not despise their prayer.

PSALM 102:17 NRSV

ENCOURAGEMENT

Once I heard a beautiful prayer, which I can never forget. It was this: "Lord, take my lips and speak through them; take my mind and think through it; take my heart and set it on fire." And this is the way the Master keeps the lips of His servants—by so filling their hearts with His love that the outflow cannot be unloving.

—FRANCES RIDLEY HAVERGAL

A CHRISTLIKE HEART REFLECTS GOD'S . . .
FAITH

For by the grace (unmerited favor of God) given to me I warn everyone among you not to estimate and think of himself more highly than he ought [not to have an exaggerated opinion of his own importance], but to rate his ability with sober judgment, each according to the degree of faith apportioned by God to him.

ROMANS 12:3 AB

With all your heart you must trust the LORD and not your own judgment. Always let him lead you, and he will clear the road for you to follow.

PROVERBS 3:5–6 CEV

My [Paul's] message and my preaching were not in persuasive words of wisdom, but in demonstration of the Spirit and of power, so that your faith would not rest on the wisdom of men, but on the power of God.

1 CORINTHIANS 2:4–5 NASB

Jesus was matter-of-fact: "Embrace this God-life. Really embrace it, … That's why I urge you to pray for absolutely everything, ranging from small to large. Include everything as you embrace this God-life, and you'll get God's everything."

MARK 11:22, 24 MSG

FAITH

Confess your sins to each other and pray for each other so God can heal you. When a believing person prays, great things happen.

JAMES 5:16 NCV

So then faith comes by hearing, and hearing by the word of God.

ROMANS 10:17 NKJV

I have been crucified with Christ. I don't live any longer. Christ lives in me. My faith in the Son of God helps me to live my life in my body. He loved me. He gave himself for me.

GALATIANS 2:20 NIRV

In addition to all this, take up the shield of faith, with which you can extinguish all the flaming arrows of the evil one.

EPHESIANS 6:16

God saved you by his special favor when you believed. And you can't take credit for this; it is a gift from God.

EPHESIANS 2:8 NLT

FAITH

That the genuineness of your faith—being more precious than gold that, though perishable, is tested by fire—may be found to result in praise and glory and honor when Jesus Christ is revealed. Although you have not seen him, you love him; and even though you do not see him now, you believe in him and rejoice with an indescribable and glorious joy, for you are receiving the outcome of your faith, the salvation of your souls.

I PETER 1:7–9 NRSV

"For truly, I say to you, if you have faith as a grain of mustard seed, you will say to this mountain, 'Move from here to there,' and it will move; and nothing will be impossible to you."

MATTHEW 17:20 RSV

"In that day you will ask me no question. Most assuredly I tell you, whatever you may ask of the Father in my name, he will give it to you. Until now, you have asked nothing in my name. Ask, and you will receive, that your joy may be made full."

JOHN 16:23–24 WEB

FAITH

It is impossible to please God without faith. Anyone who wants to come to him must believe that there is a God and that he rewards those who sincerely seek him.

HEBREWS 11:6 NLT

"I tell you the truth, anyone who has faith in me will do what I have been doing. He will do even greater things than these, because I am going to the Father."

JOHN 14:12

Look at that man, bloated by self-importance—full of himself but soul-empty. But the person in right standing before God through loyal and steady believing is fully alive, really alive.

HABAKKUK 2:4 MSG

And Jesus said to him, "'If You can?' All things are possible to him who believes." Immediately the boy's father cried out and said, "I do believe; help my unbelief."

MARK 9:23–24 NASB

Every child of God can defeat the world, and our faith is what gives us this victory.

1 JOHN 5:4 CEV

FAITH

Now God has shown us a different way of being right in his sight—not by obeying the law but by the way promised in the Scriptures long ago. We are made right in God's sight when we trust in Jesus Christ to take away our sins. And we all can be saved in this same way, no matter who we are or what we have done.

ROMANS 3:21–22 NLT

The Word is the instrumental cause of our conversion, the Spirit is the efficient ... it is the Spirit blowing in them that effectually changes the heart....
Therefore the aid of God's Spirit is to be implored, that He would put forth His powerful voice, and awaken us out of the grave of unbelief.
—THOMAS WATSON

A CHRISTLIKE HEART REFLECTS GOD'S . . .
FORGIVENESS

"Do not judge, and you will not be judged. Do not condemn, and you will not be condemned. Forgive, and you will be forgiven."

LUKE 6:37

Those who love your law have great peace and do not stumble.

PSALM 119:165 NLT

Admit to one another that you have sinned. Pray for one another so that you might be healed. The prayer of a godly person is powerful. It makes things happen.

JAMES 5:16 NIRV

Giving thanks to the Father, who has qualified us to share in the inheritance of the saints in Light. For He rescued us from the domain of darkness, and transferred us to the kingdom of His beloved Son, in whom we have redemption, the forgiveness of sins.

COLOSSIANS 1:12–14 NASB

"When you are praying, if you are angry with someone, forgive him so that your Father in heaven will also forgive your sins."

MARK 11:25 NCV

FORGIVENESS

You were dead through your trespasses and the uncircumcision of your flesh. He made you alive together with him, having forgiven us all our trespasses; having blotted out the bond written in ordinances that was against us, which was contrary to us: and he has taken it out that way, nailing it to the cross.

COLOSSIANS 2:13–14 WEB

"But that you may know that the Son of Man has authority on earth to forgive sins" (he said to the paralyzed man), "I tell you, arise, and take up your cot, and go to your house."

LUKE 5:24 WEB

"Let it be known to you therefore, my brothers, that through this man forgiveness of sins is proclaimed to you; by this Jesus everyone who believes is set free from all those sins from which you could not be freed by the law of Moses."

ACTS 13:38–39 NRSV

In Him we have redemption (deliverance and salvation) through His blood, the remission (forgiveness) of our offenses (shortcomings and trespasses), in accordance with the riches and the generosity of His gracious favor.

EPHESIANS 1:7 AB

45

FORGIVENESS

Oh, what joy for those whose disobedience is forgiven, whose sins are put out of sight.

ROMANS 4:7 NLT

Forbearing one another and, if one has a complaint against another, forgiving each other; as the Lord has forgiven you, so you also must forgive.

COLOSSIANS 3:13 RSV

And as far as sunrise is from sunset, he has separated us from our sins.

PSALM 103:12 MSG

The LORD says, "Come, let us talk about these things. Though your sins are like scarlet, they can be as white as snow. Though your sins are deep red, they can be white like wool."

ISAIAH 1:18 NCV

"I, even I, am He who blots out your transgressions for My own sake; And I will not remember your sins. Put Me in remembrance; Let us contend together; State your case, that you may be acquitted."

ISAIAH 43:25–26 NKJV

FORGIVENESS

It is cheaper to pardon than to resent. Forgiveness
saves the expense of anger, the cost of hatred.
—HANNAH MORE

47

A CHRISTLIKE HEART REFLECTS GOD'S . . .
FREEDOM

That nature (creation) itself will be set free from its bondage to decay and corruption [and gain an entrance] into the glorious freedom of God's children.

ROMANS 8:21 AB

"The Lord's Spirit has come to me, because he has chosen me to tell the good news to the poor. The Lord has sent me to announce freedom for prisoners, to give sight to the blind, to free everyone who suffers."

LUKE 4:18 CEV

One who looks intently at the perfect law, the law of liberty, and abides by it, not having become a forgetful hearer but an effectual doer, this man will be blessed in what he does.

JAMES 1:25 NASB

It is absolutely clear that God has called you to a free life. Just make sure that you don't use this freedom as an excuse to do whatever you want to do and destroy your freedom. Rather, use your freedom to serve one another in love; that's how freedom grows.

GALATIANS 5:13 MSG

FREEDOM

We have freedom now, because Christ made us free. So stand strong. Do not change and go back into the slavery of the law.

GALATIANS 5:1 NCV

Do you not know that all of us who have been baptized into Christ Jesus were baptized into his death? Therefore we have been buried with him by baptism into death, so that, just as Christ was raised from the dead by the glory of the Father, so we too might walk in newness of life.... We know that our old self was crucified with him so that the body of sin might be destroyed, and we might no longer be enslaved to sin. For whoever has died is freed from sin.

ROMANS 6:3–4, 6–7 NRSV

If the Son makes you free, you shall be free indeed.

JOHN 8:36 NKJV

"You will know the truth. And the truth will set you free."

JOHN 8:32 NIRV

I will walk about in freedom, for I have sought out your precepts.

PSALM 119:45

FREEDOM

Restore to me again the joy of your salvation, and make me willing to obey you.

PSALM 51:12 NLT

For though I am free from all men, I have made myself a slave to all, that I might win the more.

1 CORINTHIANS 9:19 RSV

Being made free from sin, you became servants of righteousness.

ROMANS 6:18 WEB

Only be careful that this power of choice (this permission and liberty to do as you please) which is yours, does not [somehow] become a hindrance (cause of stumbling) to the weak or overscrupulous [giving them an impulse to sin].

1 CORINTHIANS 8:9 AB

The Lord and the Spirit are one and the same, and the Lord's Spirit sets us free.

2 CORINTHIANS 3:17 CEV

From my distress I called upon the LORD; The LORD answered me and set me in a large place.

PSALM 118:5 NASB

FREEDOM

For the law of the Spirit of life in Christ Jesus has set me free from the law of sin and death.

ROMANS 8:2 RSV

Christ has once again made you free from the power of sin, as well as from its guilt and punishment. So do not become entangled again in the yoke of bondage.... If you have stumbled, O seeker of God, do not just lie there fretting and bemoaning your weakness! Patiently pray: "Lord, I acknowledge that every moment I would be stumbling if You were not upholding me." And then get up! Leap! Walk! Go on your way!

—**JOHN WESLEY**

A CHRISTLIKE HEART REFLECTS GOD'S . . .
FRIENDSHIP

Don't hang out with angry people; don't keep company with hotheads.

PROVERBS 22:24 MSG

A man of many companions may be ruined, But there is a friend who sticks closer than a brother.

PROVERBS 18:24 WEB

Whoever loves pure thoughts and kind words will have even the king as a friend.

PROVERBS 22:11 NCV

A friend loves at all times, and a brother is born for adversity.

PROVERBS 17:17 RSV

Whoever therefore wants to be a friend of the world makes himself an enemy of God.

JAMES 4:4 NKJV

Thus the scripture was fulfilled that says, "Abraham believed God, and it was reckoned to him as righteousness," and he was called the friend of God.

JAMES 2:23 NRSV

FRIENDSHIP

◆

As iron sharpens iron, so one person sharpens another.

PROVERBS 27:17 NIRV

Never abandon a friend—either yours or your father's. Then in your time of need, you won't have to ask your relatives for assistance. It is better to go to a neighbor than to a relative who lives far away.

PROVERBS 27:10 NLT

Wounds from a friend can be trusted, but an enemy multiplies kisses.

PROVERBS 27:6

"Servants don't know what their master is doing, and so I don't speak to you as my servants. I speak to you as my friends, and I have told you everything that my Father has told me."

JOHN 15:15 CEV

A friend is one who knows you as you are, understands where you've been, accepts who you've become, and still, gently, invites you to grow.

—UNKNOWN

53

A CHRISTLIKE HEART REFLECTS GOD'S . . .
GUIDANCE

Your ears shall hear a word behind you, saying, "This is the way, walk in it," Whenever you turn to the right hand or whenever you turn to the left.

ISAIAH 30:21 NKJV

For you will not go out with haste, nor will you go in flight [as was necessary when Israel left Egypt]; for the Lord will go before you, and the God of Israel will be your rear guard.

ISAIAH 52:12 AB

You always show me the path that leads to life. You will fill me with joy when I am with you. You will give me endless pleasures at your right hand.

PSALM 16:11 NIRV

The LORD says, "I will guide you along the best pathway for your life. I will advise you and watch over you."

PSALM 32:8 NLT

In all your ways acknowledge Him, and He will make your paths straight.

PROVERBS 3:6 NASB

GUIDANCE

Your word is a lamp for my feet and a light for my path.

PSALM 119:105 NLT

You belong. The Holy One anointed you, and you all know it.

1 JOHN 2:20 MSG

The integrity of the upright shall guide them, but the willful contrariness and crookedness of the treacherous shall destroy them.

PROVERBS 11:3 AB

People can make all kinds of plans, but only the LORD's plan will happen.

PROVERBS 19:21 NCV

We always pray that God will show you everything he wants you to do and that you may have all the wisdom and understanding that his Spirit gives. Then you will live a life that honors the Lord, and you will always please him by doing good deeds. You will come to know God even better.... I pray that you will be grateful to God for letting you have part in what he has promised his people in the kingdom of light.

COLOSSIANS 1:9–10, 12 CEV

55

GUIDANCE

That this is God, our God for ever and ever. He will be our guide for ever.

PSALM 48:14 RSV

He will guide the humble in justice. He will teach the humble his way.

PSALM 25:9 WEB

But the path of the righteous is like the light of dawn, which shines brighter and brighter until full day.

PROVERBS 4:18 NRSV

"The gatekeeper opens the gate for him, and the sheep hear his voice and come to him. He calls his own sheep by name and leads them out. After he has gathered his own flock, he walks ahead of them, and they follow him because they recognize his voice. They won't follow a stranger; they will run from him because they don't recognize his voice.... My sheep recognize my voice; I know them, and they follow me."

JOHN 10:3–5, 27 NLT

He restores my soul. He guides me in paths of righteousness for his name's sake.

PSALM 23:3

GUIDANCE

"When the Spirit of truth comes, he will guide you into all truth. He will not speak on his own. He will speak only what he hears. And he will tell you what is still going to happen."

JOHN 16:13 NIRV

I will bring the blind by a way they did not know; I will lead them in paths they have not known. I will make darkness light before them, and crooked places straight. These things I will do for them, and not forsake them.

ISAIAH 42:16 NKJV

You're my cave to hide in, my cliff to climb. Be my safe leader, be my true mountain guide.

PSALM 31:3 MSG

This is what the LORD, who saves you, the Holy One of Israel, says: "I am the LORD your God, who teaches you to do what is good, who leads you in the way you should go.

ISAIAH 48:17 NCV

GUIDANCE

God gives us his light in an instant, allowing us to know all that we need to know. No more is given to us than is necessary in his plan to lead us to perfection. We cannot seek this light; it is given to us from God only as he chooses. Neither do we know how it comes, or how we even know that it is! If we try to know more than we have been made to know, we will accomplish nothing.

—CATHERINE OF GENOA

A CHRISTLIKE HEART REFLECTS GOD'S . . .
HOPE

I pray that the God who gives hope will fill you with much joy and peace while you trust in him. Then your hope will overflow by the power of the Holy Spirit.

ROMANS 15:13 NCV

For whatever was thus written in former days was written for our instruction, that by [our steadfast and patient] endurance and the encouragement [drawn] from the Scriptures we might hold fast to and cherish hope.

ROMANS 15:4 AB

For ages and ages this message was kept secret from everyone, but now it has been explained to God's people. God did this because he wanted you Gentiles to understand his wonderful and glorious mystery. And the mystery is that Christ lives in you, and he is your hope of sharing in God's glory.

COLOSSIANS 1:26–27 CEV

If we have hoped in Christ in this life only, we are of all men most to be pitied. But now Christ has been raised from the dead, the first fruits of those who are asleep.

1 CORINTHIANS 15:19–20 NASB

HOPE

Remember what you said to me, your servant—I hang on to these words for dear life! These words hold me up in bad times; yes, your promises rejuvenate me.

PSALM 119:49–50 MSG

Behold, the eye of the LORD is on those who fear Him, on those who hope in His mercy, to deliver their soul from death, and to keep them alive in famine.

PSALM 33:18–19 NKJV

I say to myself, "The LORD is my portion; therefore I will wait for him." The LORD is good to those whose hope is in him, to the one who seeks him; it is good to wait quietly for the salvation of the LORD.

LAMENTATIONS 3:24–26

Our soul has waited for [the Lord]. He is our help and our shield. For our heart shall rejoice in him, because we have trusted in his holy name. Let your lovingkindness be on us, [God] since we have hoped in you.

PSALM 33:20–22 WEB

Lord, I wait for you to help me. Lord my God, I know you will answer.

PSALM 38:15 NIRV

HOPE

Having been justified by his grace, we might become heirs having the hope of eternal life.

TITUS 3:7

Through him we have obtained access to this grace in which we stand, and we rejoice in our hope of sharing the glory of God.

ROMANS 5:2 RSV

For you, O Lord, are my hope, my trust, O Lord, from my youth…. I will hope continually, and will praise you yet more and more.

PSALM 71:5, 14 NRSV

And this hope is what saves us. But if we already have what we hope for, there is no need to keep on hoping. However, we hope for something we have not yet seen, and we patiently wait for it.

ROMANS 8:24–25 CEV

Since we heard of your faith in Christ Jesus and of your love for all the saints; because of the hope which is laid up for you in heaven, of which you heard before in the word of the truth of the gospel.

COLOSSIANS 1:4–5 NKJV

HOPE

In the same way God, desiring even more to show to the heirs of the promise the unchangeableness of His purpose, interposed with an oath, so that by two unchangeable things in which it is impossible for God to lie, we who have taken refuge would have strong encouragement to take hold of the hope set before us. This hope we have as an anchor of the soul, a hope both sure and steadfast and one which enters within the veil.

HEBREWS 6:17–19 NASB

I have set the LORD always before me. Because he is at my right hand, I will not be shaken. Therefore my heart is glad and my tongue rejoices; my body also will rest secure.

PSALM 16:8–9

Why are you down in the dumps, dear soul? Why are you crying the blues? Fix my eyes on God—soon I'll be praising again. He puts a smile on my face. He's my God.

PSALM 42:11 MSG

Let those who respect you rejoice when they see me, because I put my hope in your word.

PSALM 119:74 NCV

HOPE

We share the sufferings of Christ. We also share his comfort.

2 CORINTHIANS 1:5 NIRV

That you were at that time separate from Christ, alienated from the commonwealth of Israel, and strangers from the covenants of the promise, having no hope and without God in the world. But now in Christ Jesus you who once were far off are made near in the blood of Christ.

EPHESIANS 2:12–13 WEB

O hope! Dazzling, radiant hope! What a change thou bringest to the hopeless; brightening the darkened paths, and cheering the lonely way.

—AIMEE SEMPLE MCPHERSON

A CHRISTLIKE HEART REFLECTS GOD'S . . .
INTEGRITY

Lord, judge the people. Lord, defend me because I am right, because I have done no wrong, God Most High. God, you do what is right. You know our thoughts and feelings. Stop those wicked actions done by evil people, and help those who do what is right. God protects me like a shield; he saves those whose hearts are right.

PSALM 7:8–10 NCV

An honest person tells the truth in court, but a dishonest person tells nothing but lies.... The LORD hates every liar, but he is the friend of all who can be trusted.

PROVERBS 12:17, 22 CEV

For the word of the LORD holds true, and everything he does is worthy of our trust. He loves whatever is just and good, and his unfailing love fills the earth.

PSALM 33:4–5 NLT

He who walks in integrity walks securely, but he who perverts his ways will be found out.

PROVERBS 10:9 RSV

The integrity of the upright will guide them, but the perversity of the unfaithful will destroy them.

PROVERBS 11:3 NKJV

INTEGRITY

The Rock, his work is perfect; for all his ways are justice: a God of faithfulness and without iniquity, just and right is he.

DEUTERONOMY 32:4 WEB

The mouths of the righteous (those harmonious with God) bring forth skillful and godly Wisdom, but the perverse tongue shall be cut down [like a barren and rotten tree].

PROVERBS 10:31 AB

He will cover you with his feathers, and under his wings you will find refuge; his faithfulness will be your shield and rampart.

PSALM 91:4

Behold, You desire truth in the innermost being, and in the hidden part You will make me know wisdom.

PSALM 51:6 NASB

A God-loyal life keeps you on track; sin dumps the wicked in the ditch.

PROVERBS 13:6 MSG

A person who lives right and is right has more power in his silence than another has by words. Character is like bells, which ring out sweet notes and which, when touched—accidentally even—resound with sweet music.
—PHILLIPS BROOKS

A CHRISTLIKE HEART REFLECTS GOD'S . . .
JOY

The afflicted also will increase their gladness in the LORD, and the needy of mankind will rejoice in the Holy One of Israel.

ISAIAH 29:19 NASB

You have turned my sorrow into joyful dancing. No longer am I sad and wearing sackcloth. I thank you from my heart, and I will never stop singing your praises, my LORD and my God.

PSALM 30:11–12 CEV

He makes the barren woman to be a homemaker and a joyful mother of [spiritual] children. Praise the Lord! (Hallelujah!)

PSALM 113:9 AB

"If you keep my commandments, you will abide in my love, just as I have kept my Father's commandments and abide in his love. These things I have spoken to you, that my joy may be in you, and that your joy may be full."

JOHN 15:10–11 RSV

A glad heart makes a cheerful face; but an aching heart breaks the spirit.

PROVERBS 15:13 WEB

JOY

A miserable heart means a miserable life; a cheerful heart fills the day with song.

PROVERBS 15:15 MSG

You will live in joy and peace. The mountains and hills will burst into song, and the trees of the field will clap their hands!

ISAIAH 55:12 NLT

For the kingdom of God is not a matter of eating and drinking, but of righteousness, peace and joy in the Holy Spirit.

ROMANS 14:17

You will show me the path of life; in Your presence is fullness of joy; at Your right hand are pleasures forevermore.

PSALM 16:11 NKJV

Now we are also very happy in God through our Lord Jesus Christ. Through him we are now God's friends again.

ROMANS 5:11 NCV

A cheerful disposition is good for your health; gloom and doom leave you bone-tired.

PROVERBS 17:22 MSG

JOY

For You, O LORD, have made me glad by what You have done, I will sing for joy at the works of Your hands. How great are Your works, O LORD! Your thoughts are very deep.

PSALM 92:4–5 NASB

With all my heart, I will praise the LORD. Let all who are helpless, listen and be glad.

PSALM 34:2 CEV

The joy of the Lord is your strength and stronghold.

NEHEMIAH 8:10 AB

*Eternal bliss is rooted in God alone and nothing else.
And if people are to be saved, this one and only God
must be in their soul.... For bliss or blessedness does
not come from the wealth of things, but from God.
In other words, bliss or blessedness does not depend
on any created thing or on a creature's work, but only
on God and His works.*

—THEOLOGIA GERMANICA

69

LEADERSHIP

Every morning you'll hear me at it again. Every morning I lay out the pieces of my life on your altar and watch for fire to descend. Waiting for directions to get me safely through enemy lines.

PSALM 5:3, 8 MSG

The LORD is my shepherd; I have everything I need. He lets me rest in green pastures. He leads me to calm water. He gives me new strength. He leads me on paths that are right for the good of his name.

PSALM 23:1–3 NCV

From the end of the earth I will cry to You, When my heart is overwhelmed; lead me to the rock that is higher than I. For You have been a shelter for me, a strong tower from the enemy.

PSALM 61:2–3 NKJV

Since you are my rock and my fortress, for the sake of your name lead and guide me.

PSALM 31:3

Keep us from being tempted and protect us from evil.

MATTHEW 6:13 CEV

LEADERSHIP

O LORD, you have examined my heart and know everything about me. You know when I sit down or stand up. You know my every thought when far away.... I can never escape from your spirit! I can never get away from your presence! If I go up to heaven, you are there; if I go down to the place of the dead, you are there. If I ride the wings of the morning, if I dwell by the farthest oceans, even there your hand will guide me, and your strength will support me.

PSALM 139:1–2, 7–10 NLT

Let me hear of your steadfast love in the morning, for in you I put my trust. Teach me the way I should go, for to you I lift up my soul. Save me, O Lord, from my enemies; I have fled to you for refuge. Teach me to do your will, for you are my God. Let your good spirit lead me on a level path.

PSALM 143:8–10 NRSV

Behold, the Lord GOD comes with might, and his arm rules for him; behold, his reward is with him, and his recompense before him. He will feed his flock like a shepherd, he will gather the lambs in his arms, he will carry them in his bosom, and gently lead those that are with young.

ISAIAH 40:10–11 RSV

LEADERSHIP

"I will bring the blind by a way that they don't know; in paths that they don't know will I lead them; I will make darkness light before them, and crooked places straight. These things will I do, and I will not forsake them."

ISAIAH 42:16 WEB

Thus says the Lord, your Redeemer, the Holy One of Israel: I am the Lord your God, Who teaches you to profit, Who leads you in the way that you should go.

ISAIAH 48:17 AB

Lead me in Your truth and teach me, for You are the God of my salvation; for You I wait all the day.

PSALM 25:5 NASB

I set him up as a witness to the nations, made him a prince and leader of the nations.

ISAIAH 55:4 MSG

LEADERSHIP

My son, keep your father's commands, and don't forget your mother's teaching. Keep their words in mind forever as though you had them tied around your neck. They will guide you when you walk. They will guard you when you sleep. They will speak to you when you are awake. These commands are like a lamp; this teaching is like a light. And the correction that comes from them will help you have life.

PROVERBS 6:20–23 NCV

"I [Wisdom] traverse the way of righteousness, in the midst of the paths of justice, that I may cause those who love me to inherit wealth, that I may fill their treasuries."

PROVERBS 8:20–21 NKJV

Do you wish to rise? Begin by descending. You plan a tower that shall pierce the clouds? Lay first the foundation of humility!
—**AUGUSTINE OF HIPPO**

A CHRISTLIKE HEART REFLECTS GOD'S . . .
LOVE

Hatred stirs up dissension, but love covers over all wrongs.

PROVERBS 10:12

We know that we have passed out of death into life, because
we love the brothers. He who doesn't love his brother remains
in death.

1 JOHN 3:14 WEB

Love is patient and kind; love is not jealous or boastful; it is
not arrogant or rude. Love does not insist on its own way; it
is not irritable or resentful; it does not rejoice at wrong, but
rejoices in the right. Love bears all things, believes all things,
hopes all things, endures all things. Love never ends.

1 CORINTHIANS 13:4–8 RSV

"I tell you, love your enemies. Help and give without expect-
ing a return. You'll never—I promise—regret it. Live out this
God-created identity the way our Father lives toward us, generously and graciously, even when we're at our worst."

LUKE 6:35 MSG

Whoever does not love does not know God, because God is
love.

1 JOHN 4:8 NCV

LOVE

"So now I am giving you a new commandment: Love each other. Just as I have loved you, you should love each other. Your love for one another will prove to the world that you are my disciples."

JOHN 13:34–35 NLT

I am sure that nothing can separate us from God's love—not life or death, not angels or spirits, not the present or the future, and not powers above or powers below. Nothing in all creation can separate us from God's love for us in Christ Jesus our Lord!

ROMANS 8:38–39 CEV

Yet the Lord will command His loving-kindness in the day-time, and in the night His song shall be with me, a prayer to the God of my life.

PSALM 42:8 AB

The God of Israel, there is no God like you, in heaven, or on earth; who keep covenant and lovingkindness with your servants, who walk before you with all their heart.

2 CHRONICLES 6:14 WEB

LOVE

Those who spare the rod hate their children, but those who love them are diligent to discipline them.

PROVERBS 13:24 NRSV

And the most important piece of clothing you must wear is love. Love is what binds us all together in perfect harmony.

COLOSSIANS 3:14 NLT

Because of his great love for us, God, who is rich in mercy, made us alive with Christ even when we were dead in transgressions—it is by grace you have been saved.

EPHESIANS 2:4–5

By this we know love, because He laid down His life for us. And we also ought to lay down our lives for the brethren.

1 JOHN 3:16 NKJV

And this hope will never disappoint us, because God has poured out his love to fill our hearts. He gave us his love through the Holy Spirit, whom God has given to us.

ROMANS 5:5 NCV

What marvelous love the Father has extended to us! Just look at it—we're called children of God! That's who we really are.

1 JOHN 3:1 MSG

LOVE

For God so loved the world, that He gave His only begotten Son, that whoever believes in Him shall not perish, but have eternal life.

JOHN 3:16 NASB

God is love. If we keep on loving others, we will stay one in our hearts with God, and he will stay one with us.

1 JOHN 4:16 CEV

If God loved us so, we also ought to love one another.

1 JOHN 4:11 WEB

The LORD appeared to him from afar. I have loved you with an everlasting love; therefore I have continued my faithfulness to you.

JEREMIAH 31:3 RSV

Let us love one another, because love is from God; everyone who loves is born of God and knows God.

1 JOHN 4:7 NRSV

LOVE

And may you have the power to understand, as all God's people should, how wide, how long, how high, and how deep his love really is. May you experience the love of Christ, though it is so great you will never fully understand it. Then you will be filled with the fullness of life and power that comes from God. Now glory be to God! By his mighty power at work within us, he is able to accomplish infinitely more than we would ever dare to ask or hope.

EPHESIANS 3:18–20 NLT

Very rarely will anyone die for a righteous man, though for a good man someone might possibly dare to die. But God demonstrates his own love for us in this: While we were still sinners, Christ died for us.

ROMANS 5:7–8

Let your religion be less of a theory and more of a love affair.
—G. K. CHESTERTON

A CHRISTLIKE HEART REFLECTS GOD'S . . .
LOYALTY

He hates sinful people. He honors those who have respect for the Lord. He keeps his promises even when it hurts.

PSALM 15:4 NIRV

"I will in no way leave you, neither will I in any way forsake you."

HEBREWS 13:5 WEB

No one has greater love [no one has shown stronger affection] than to lay down (give up) his own life for his friends.

JOHN 15:13 AB

"I will tell you the kind of special day I want: Free the people you have put in prison unfairly and undo their chains. Free those to whom you are unfair and stop their hard labor. Share your food with the hungry and bring poor, homeless people into your own homes. When you see someone who has no clothes, give him yours, and don't refuse to help your own relatives."

ISAIAH 58:6–7 NCV

Love does not demand its own way. Love is not irritable, and it keeps no record of when it has been wronged. It is never glad about injustice but rejoices whenever the truth wins out.

Love never gives up, never loses faith, is always hopeful, and endures through every circumstance. Love will last forever.

I CORINTHIANS 13:5–8 NLT

I will speak ill of no man and speak all the good I know of everybody.
—BENJAMIN FRANKLIN

A CHRISTLIKE HEART REFLECTS GOD'S . . .
MERCY

Guilt is banished through love and truth; Fear-of-GOD deflects evil.

PROVERBS 16:6 MSG

He saved us, not on the basis of deeds which we have done in righteousness, but according to His mercy, by the washing of regeneration and renewing by the Holy Spirit.

TITUS 3:5 NASB

Praised (honored, blessed) be the God and Father of our Lord Jesus Christ (the Messiah)! By His boundless mercy we have been born again to an ever-living hope through the resurrection of Jesus Christ from the dead.

1 PETER 1:3 AB

We have a great high priest, who has gone into heaven, and he is Jesus the Son of God. That is why we must hold on to what we have said about him. Jesus understands every weakness of ours, because he was tempted in every way that we are. But he did not sin! So whenever we are in need, we should come bravely before the throne of our merciful God. There we will be treated with undeserved kindness, and we will find help.

HEBREWS 4:14–16 CEV

MERCY

Love and faithfulness keep the king safe. His throne is sustained by love.

PROVERBS 20:28 WEB

He who despises his neighbor is a sinner, but happy is he who is kind to the poor.

PROVERBS 14:21 RSV

They shall not hunger or thirst, neither scorching wind nor sun shall strike them down, for he who has pity on them will lead them, and by springs of water will guide them.

ISAIAH 49:10 NRSV

I said, "Plant the good seeds of righteousness, and you will harvest a crop of my love. Plow up the hard ground of your hearts, for now is the time to seek the LORD, that he may come and shower righteousness upon you."

HOSEA 10:12 NLT

Because of the tender mercy of our God, by which the rising sun will come to us from heaven to shine on those living in darkness and in the shadow of death, to guide our feet into the path of peace.

LUKE 1:78–79

MERCY

Yes, [Jacob] struggled with the Angel and prevailed; he wept, and sought favor from Him. He found Him in Bethel, and there He spoke to us—that is, the Lord God of hosts. The Lord is His memorable name. So you, by the help of your God, return; observe mercy and justice, and wait on your God continually.

HOSEA 12:4–6 NKJV

Those who show mercy to others are happy, because God will show mercy to them.

MATTHEW 5:7 NCV

Let love and loyalty always show like a necklace, and write them in your mind. God and people will like you and consider you a success.

PROVERBS 3:3–4 CEV

He who earnestly seeks after and craves righteousness, mercy, and loving-kindness will find life in addition to righteousness (uprightness and right standing with God) and honor.

PROVERBS 21:21 AB

MERCY

His mercy is for generations of generations on those who fear him.

LUKE 1:50 WEB

The LORD is merciful and gracious, slow to anger and abounding in steadfast love.

PSALM 103:8 RSV

I said, "O Lord God of heaven, the great and awesome God who keeps covenant and steadfast love with those who love him and keep his commandments; let your ear be attentive and your eyes open to hear the prayer of your servant that I now pray before you day and night for your servants, the people of Israel, confessing the sins of the people of Israel, which we have sinned against you. Both I and my family have sinned.

NEHEMIAH 1:5–6 NRSV

Let the wicked abandon their way of life and the evil their way of thinking. Let them come back to GOD, who is merciful, come back to our God, who is lavish with forgiveness.

ISAIAH 55:7 MSG

MERCY

"Be merciful, just as your Father is merciful. Do not judge, and you will not be judged; and do not condemn, and you will not be condemned; pardon, and you will be pardoned."

LUKE 6:36–37 NASB

O people, the LORD has already told you what is good, and this is what he requires: to do what is right, to love mercy, and to walk humbly with your God.

MICAH 6:8 NLT

Remember, O LORD, your great mercy and love, for they are from of old.

PSALM 25:6

Mercy comes down from heaven to earth so that one,
by practicing it, may resemble God.
—GIAMBATTISTA GIRALDI

A CHRISTLIKE HEART REFLECTS GOD'S . . .
OPTIMISM

This is the message he has given us to announce to you: God is light and there is no darkness in him at all.

1 JOHN 1:5 NLT

We know that all things work together for good for those who love God, who are called according to his purpose.

ROMANS 8:28 NRSV

I lift up my eyes to the hills. From whence does my help come? My help comes from the LORD, who made heaven and earth.

PSALM 121:1–2 RSV

I know how to be humbled, and I know also how to abound. In everything and in all things have I learned the secret both to be filled and to be hungry, both to abound and to be in need.

PHILIPPIANS 4:12 WEB

Always be glad because of the Lord! I will say it again: Be glad.... Don't worry about anything, but pray about everything. With thankful hearts offer up your prayers and requests to God.

PHILIPPIANS 4:4, 6 CEV

OPTIMISM

And God is able to make all grace (every favor and earthly blessing) come to you in abundance, so that you may always and under all circumstances and whatever the need be self-sufficient [possessing enough to require no aid or support and furnished in abundance for every good work and charitable donation].

2 CORINTHIANS 9:8 AB

Thanks be to God, who always leads us in triumph in Christ, and manifests through us the sweet aroma of the knowledge of Him in every place.

2 CORINTHIANS 2:14 NASB

Listen to my voice in the morning, LORD. Each morning I bring my requests to you and wait expectantly.

PSALM 5:3 NLT

"And then—then!—they'll see the Son of Man welcomed in grand style—a glorious welcome! When all this starts to happen, up on your feet. Stand tall with your heads high. Help is on the way!"

LUKE 21:27–28 MSG

OPTIMISM

Lord, you give light to my lamp. My God brightens the darkness around me. With your help I can attack an army. With God's help I can jump over a wall.

PSALM 18:28–29 NCV

All things shall be well and all shall be well, and all manner of things shall be well.

—JULIAN OF NORWICH

A CHRISTLIKE HEART REFLECTS GOD'S . . .
PEACE

Peace I leave with you, my peace I give to you; not as the world gives do I give to you. Let not your heart be troubled, neither let it be afraid.

JOHN 14:27 NKJV

The Lord is my shepherd. He gives me everything I need. He lets me lie down in fields of green grass. He leads me beside quiet waters.

PSALM 23:1–2 NIRV

He ransoms me unharmed from the battle waged against me, even though many oppose me.

PSALM 55:18

All this newness of life is from God, who brought us back to himself through what Christ did. And God has given us the task of reconciling people to him. For God was in Christ, reconciling the world to himself, no longer counting people's sins against them. This is the wonderful message he has given us to tell others.

2 CORINTHIANS 5:18–19 NLT

PEACE

The effect of righteousness will be peace, and the result of righteousness, quietness and trust forever. My people will abide in a peaceful habitation, in secure dwellings, and in quiet resting places.

ISAIAH 32:17–18 NRSV

Have no anxiety about anything, but in everything by prayer and supplication with thanksgiving let your requests be made known to God. And the peace of God, which passes all understanding, will keep your hearts and your minds in Christ Jesus.

PHILIPPIANS 4:6–7 RSV

For if, while we were enemies, we were reconciled to God through the death of his Son, much more, being reconciled, we will be saved by his life.

ROMANS 5:10 WEB

Let be and be still, and know (recognize and understand) that I am God. I will be exalted among the nations! I will be exalted in the earth!

PSALM 46:10 AB

PEACE

You know the teachings I gave you, and you know what you heard me say and saw me do. So follow my example. And God, who gives peace, will be with you.

PHILIPPIANS 4:9 CEV

Therefore, having been justified by faith, we have peace with God through our Lord Jesus Christ.

ROMANS 5:1 NASB

Obsession with self in these matters is a dead end; attention to God leads us out into the open, into a spacious, free life.

ROMANS 8:6 MSG

"The mountains may disappear, and the hills may come to an end, but my love will never disappear; my promise of peace will not come to an end," says the LORD who shows mercy to you.

ISAIAH 54:10 NCV

[Jesus] was wounded for our transgressions, he was bruised for our iniquities; the chastisement for our peace was upon Him, and by His stripes we are healed.

ISAIAH 53:5 NKJV

PEACE

Think about those who are without blame. Look at those who are honest. A man who loves peace will have a tomorrow.

PSALM 37:37 NIRV

For God is not a God of disorder but of peace. As in all the congregations of the saints.

I CORINTHIANS 14:33

Blessed are the peacemakers: for they shall be called the children of God.

MATTHEW 5:9 KJV

Deceit is in the mind of those who plan evil, but those who counsel peace have joy.

PROVERBS 12:20 NRSV

You will keep [him] in perfect peace, [whose] mind [is] stayed [on you]; because he trusts in you.

ISAIAH 26:3 WEB

Peace, peace, to the far and to the near, says the LORD; and I will heal him.

ISAIAH 57:19 RSV

And the harvest of righteousness (of conformity to God's will

PEACE

in thought and deed) is [the fruit of the seed] sown in peace by those who work for and make peace [in themselves and in others, that peace which means concord, agreement, and harmony between individuals, with undisturbedness, in a peaceful mind free from fears and agitating passions and moral conflicts].

JAMES 3:18 AB

True peace is found by man in the depths of his own heart, the swelling-place of God.
—**JOHANN TAULER**

PERSEVERANCE

Stand firm, and hold the traditions which you were taught by us, whether by word, or by letter. Now our Lord Jesus Christ himself, and God, our Father, who loved us and gave us eternal comfort and good hope through grace, comfort your hearts and establish you in every good work and word.

2 THESSALONIANS 2:15–17 WEB

For freedom Christ has set us free. Stand firm, therefore, and do not submit again to a yoke of slavery.

GALATIANS 5:1 NRSV

We give great honor to those who endure under suffering. Job is an example of a man who endured patiently. From his experience we see how the Lord's plan finally ended in good, for he is full of tenderness and mercy.

JAMES 5:11 NLT

Wait for the LORD; be strong and take heart and wait for the LORD.

PSALM 27:14

And the Master, God, stays right there and helps me, so I'm not disgraced. Therefore I set my face like flint, confident that I'll never regret this.

ISAIAH 50:7 MSG

PERSEVERANCE

Control yourselves. Be on your guard. Your enemy the devil is like a roaring lion. He prowls around looking for someone to chew up and swallow. Stand up to him. Stand firm in what you believe. All over the world you know that your brothers and sisters are going through the same kind of suffering.

I Peter 5:8–9 nirv

Therefore, my beloved brethren, be steadfast, immovable, always abounding in the work of the Lord, knowing that your labor is not in vain in the Lord.

I Corinthians 15:58 nkjv

We all share in Christ if we keep till the end the sure faith we had in the beginning.

Hebrews 3:14 ncv

"But you, be strong and do not lose courage, for there is reward for your work."

2 Chronicles 15:7 nasb

PERSEVERANCE

Save me, God, by your power and prove that I am right.
Listen to my prayer and hear what I say. Cruel strangers have
attacked and want me dead. Not one of them cares about
you. You will help me, Lord God, and keep me from falling.

PSALM 54:1–4 CEV

We are hedged in (pressed) on every side [troubled and
oppressed in every way], but not cramped or crushed; we suffer embarrassments and are perplexed and unable to find a
way out, but not driven to despair; we are pursued (persecuted and hard driven), but not deserted [to stand alone]; we are
struck down to the ground, but never struck out and
destroyed; always carrying about in the body the liability and
exposure to the same putting to death that the Lord Jesus suffered, so that the [resurrection] life of Jesus also may be
shown forth by and in our bodies. For we who live are constantly [experiencing] being handed over to death for Jesus'
sake, that the [resurrection] life of Jesus also may be evi-
denced through our flesh which is liable to death.

2 CORINTHIANS 4:8–11 AB

Nothing great was ever done without much enduring.
—CATHERINE OF SIENA

A CHRISTLIKE HEART REFLECTS GOD'S . . .
PRAYER

Build yourselves up in your most holy faith and pray in the Holy Spirit. Keep yourselves in God's love as you wait for the mercy of our Lord Jesus Christ to bring you to eternal life.

JUDE VV. 20–21

The earnest prayer of a righteous person has great power and wonderful results.

JAMES 5:16 NLT

I urge that supplications, prayers, intercessions, and thanksgivings be made for everyone, for kings and all who are in high positions, so that we may lead a quiet and peaceable life in all godliness and dignity. This is right and is acceptable in the sight of God our Savior, who desires everyone to be saved and to come to the knowledge of the truth.

1 TIMOTHY 2:1–4 NRSV

You know that the LORD has chosen for himself those who are loyal to him. The LORD listens when I pray to him.

PSALM 4:3 NCV

For the eyes of the Lord are on the righteous, and his ears open to their prayer; but the face of the Lord is against those who do evil.

1 PETER 3:12 WEB

PRAYER

But the end and culmination of all things has now come near; keep sound minded and self-restrained and alert therefore for [the practice of] prayer.

I PETER 4:7 AB

Have no anxiety about anything, but in everything by prayer and supplication with thanksgiving let your requests be made known to God. And the peace of God, which passes all understanding, will keep your hearts and your minds in Christ Jesus.

PHILIPPIANS 4:6–7 RSV

In certain ways we are weak, but the Spirit is here to help us. For example, when we don't know what to pray for, the Spirit prays for us in ways that cannot be put into words. All of our thoughts are known to God. He can understand what is in the mind of the Spirit, as the Spirit prays for God's people.

ROMANS 8:26–27 CEV

We are ambassadors for Christ, as though God were making an appeal through us; we beg you on behalf of Christ, be reconciled to God. He made Him who knew no sin to be sin on our behalf, so that we might become the righteousness of God in Him.

2 CORINTHIANS 5:20–21 NASB

PRAYER

Believing-prayer will heal you, and Jesus will put you on your feet. And if you've sinned, you'll be forgiven—healed inside and out.

JAMES 5:15 MSG

LORD, You have heard the desire of the humble; You will prepare their heart; You will cause Your ear to hear.

PSALM 10:17 NKJV

Finally, brothers and sisters, pray for us. Pray that the Lord's message will spread quickly. Pray that others will honor it just as you did. And pray that we will be saved from sinful and evil people. Not everyone is a believer. But the Lord is faithful. He will strengthen you. He will guard you from the evil one.

2 THESSALONIANS 3:1–3 NIRV

There is nothing that makes us love a man so much as praying for him.
—WILLIAM LAW

SELF-CONTROL

Keep vigilant watch over your heart; that's where life starts.

PROVERBS 4:23 MSG

"And everyone will hate you because of your allegiance to me. But not a hair of your head will perish! By standing firm, you will win your souls."

LUKE 21:17–19 NLT

Better is the end of a thing than its beginning; the patient in spirit are better than the proud in spirit. Do not be quick to anger, for anger lodges in the bosom of fools.

ECCLESIASTES 7:8–9 NRSV

He who is slow to anger has great understanding, but he who has a hasty temper exalts folly.

PROVERBS 14:29 RSV

But the fruit of the Spirit is love, joy, peace, patience, kindness, goodness, faithfulness, gentleness, and self-control. Against such things there is no law.

GALATIANS 5:22–23 WEB

Even dunces who keep quiet are thought to be wise; as long as they keep their mouths shut, they're smart.

PROVERBS 17:28 MSG

SELF-CONTROL

Understand [this], my beloved brethren. Let every man be quick to hear [a ready listener], slow to speak, slow to take offense and to get angry. For man's anger does not promote the righteousness God [wishes and requires].

JAMES 1:19–20 AB

Watching what you say can save you a lot of trouble.

PROVERBS 21:23 CEV

"For out of the overflow of the heart the mouth speaks. The good man brings good things out of the good stored up in him, and the evil man brings evil things out of the evil stored up in him.… For by your words you will be acquitted, and by your words you will be condemned."

MATTHEW 12:34–35, 37

"I will guard my ways that I may not sin with my tongue; I will guard my mouth as with a muzzle while the wicked are in my presence."

PSALM 39:1 NASB

For if you live according to the flesh you will die; but if by the Spirit you put to death the deeds of the body, you will live.

ROMANS 8:13 NKJV

101

SELF-CONTROL

Those who belong to Christ Jesus have crucified their own sinful selves. They have given up their old selfish feelings and the evil things they wanted to do. We get our new life from the Spirit, so we should follow the Spirit.

GALATIANS 5:24–25 NCV

They refused to listen to you.... But you are a God who forgives. You are gracious. You are tender and kind. You are slow to get angry. You are full of love. So you didn't desert them.

NEHEMIAH 9:17 NIRV

In this way, love is made complete among us so that we will have confidence on the day of judgment, because in this world we are like him.

1 JOHN 4:17

It is foolish to belittle a neighbor; a person with good sense remains silent.

PROVERBS 11:12 NLT

Lord of himself, though not of lands; and having nothing, yet hath all.
—**SIR HENRY WOTTON**

102

A CHRISTLIKE HEART REFLECTS GOD'S . . .
STRENGTH

The LORD is my strength and shield. I trust him, and he helps me. I am very happy, and I praise him with my song. The Lord is powerful; he gives victory to his chosen one.

PSALM 28:7–8 NCV

GOD's my strength, he's also my song, and now he's my salvation.

PSALM 118:14 MSG

And He has said to me, "My grace is sufficient for you, for power is perfected in weakness." Most gladly, therefore, I will rather boast about my weaknesses, so that the power of Christ may dwell in me. Therefore I am well content with weaknesses, with insults, with distresses, with persecutions, with difficulties, for Christ's sake; for when I am weak, then I am strong.

2 CORINTHIANS 12:9–10 NASB

The LORD protects everyone who lives right, but he destroys anyone who does wrong.

PROVERBS 10:29 CEV

Now I know that the Lord saves His anointed; He will answer him from His holy heaven with the saving strength of

STRENGTH

His right hand. Some trust in and boast of chariots and some of horses, but we will trust in and boast of the name of the Lord our God.

PSALM 20:6–7 AB

To you, my strength, I will sing praises. For God is my high tower, the God of my mercy.

PSALM 59:17 WEB

This God is my strong refuge, and has made my way safe.

2 SAMUEL 22:33 RSV

Be strong in the Lord and in the strength of his power. Put on the whole armor of God, so that you may be able to stand against the wiles of the devil.

EPHESIANS 6:10–11 NRSV

May the words of my mouth and the thoughts of my heart be pleasing to you, O LORD, my rock and my redeemer.

PSALM 19:14 NLT

The salvation of the righteous comes from the LORD; he is their stronghold in time of trouble.

PSALM 37:39

STRENGTH

Be strong and brave.... The Lord himself will go ahead of you. He will be with you. He will never leave you. He'll never desert you. So don't be afraid. Don't lose hope.

DEUTERONOMY 31:7–8 NIRV

You have armed me with strength for the battle; You have subdued under me those who rose against me.

2 SAMUEL 22:40 NKJV

Riches and honor come from you. You rule everything. You have the power and strength to make anyone great and strong.

I CHRONICLES 29:12 NCV

Counting on GOD's Rule to prevail, I take heart and gain strength. I run like a deer. I feel like I'm king of the mountain!

HABAKKUK 3:19 MSG

The foolishness of God is wiser than men, and the weakness of God is stronger than men.

I CORINTHIANS 1:25 NASB

STRENGTH

Be on your guard and stay awake. Your enemy, the devil, is like a roaring lion, sneaking around to find someone to attack. But you must resist the devil and stay strong in your faith. You know that all over the world the Lord's followers are suffering just as you are.

1 PETER 5:8–9 CEV

Have not I commanded you? Be strong, vigorous, and very courageous. Be not afraid, neither be dismayed, for the Lord your God is with you wherever you go.

JOSHUA 1:9 AB

The Lord gives strength to his people. The Lord blesses his people with peace.

PSALM 29:11 NIRV

For the eyes of the LORD run to and fro throughout the whole earth, to show his might in behalf of those whose heart is blameless toward him. You have done foolishly in this; for from now on you will have wars.

2 CHRONICLES 16:9 RSV

Incline your ear to me; rescue me speedily. Be a rock of refuge for me, a strong fortress to save me. You are indeed my rock and my fortress; for your name's sake lead me and guide me.

PSALM 31:2–3 NRSV

Honor and majesty surround him; strength and beauty are in his dwelling.

1 CHRONICLES 16:27 NLT

It was not by their sword that they won the land, nor did their arm bring them victory; it was your right hand, your arm, and the light of your face, for you loved them.... Through you we push back our enemies; through your name we trample our foes.

PSALM 44:3, 5

So let it be in God's own might
We gird us for the coming fight,
And, strong in him whose cause is ours,
In conflict with unholy powers,
We grasp the weapons he has given,
The light and truth and love of heaven.
—JOHN GREENLEAF WHITTIER

A CHRISTLIKE HEART REFLECTS GOD'S . . .
SUCCESS

Always remember what is written in the Book of the Teachings. Study it day and night to be sure to obey everything that is written there. If you do this, you will be wise and successful in everything.

JOSHUA 1:8 NCV

Now it shall come to pass, if you diligently obey the voice of the LORD your God, to observe carefully all His commandments which I command you today, that the LORD your God will set you high above all nations of the earth. And all these blessings shall come upon you and overtake you, because you obey the voice of the LORD your God.... The LORD will command the blessing on you in your storehouses and in all to which you set your hand, and He will bless you in the land which the LORD your God is giving you.

DEUTERONOMY 28:1–2, 8 NKJV

Anyone who refuses to work doesn't even cook what he catches. But a man who works hard values what he has.

PROVERBS 12:27 NIRV

Lazy hands make a man poor, but diligent hands bring wealth.

PROVERBS 10:4

SUCCESS

Work hard and become a leader; be lazy and become a slave.

PROVERBS 12:24 NLT

Those who love me, I will deliver; I will protect those who know my name.

PSALM 91:14 NRSV

Blessed is the one who obeys the law of the Lord. He doesn't follow the advice of evil people. He doesn't make a habit of doing what sinners do. He doesn't join those who make fun of the Lord and his law. Instead, he takes delight in the law of the Lord. He thinks about his law day and night. He is like a tree that is planted near a stream of water. It always bears its fruit at the right time. Its leaves don't dry up. Everything godly people do turns out well.

PSALM 1:1–3 NIRV

For not from the east nor from the west nor from the south come promotion and lifting up. But God is the Judge! He puts down one and lifts up another.

PSALM 75:6–7 AB

SUCCESS

Behold, what I have seen to be good and to be fitting is to eat and drink and find enjoyment in all the toil with which one toils under the sun the few days of his life which God has given him, for this is his lot. Every man also to whom God has given wealth and possessions and power to enjoy them, and to accept his lot and find enjoyment in his toil—this is the gift of God.

ECCLESIASTES 5:18–19 RSV

Who aimeth at the sky
Shoots higher much than he that means a tree.
—GEORGE HERBERT

A CHRISTLIKE HEART REFLECTS GOD'S . . .
THANKSGIVING

I exhort therefore, first of all, that petitions, prayers, intercessions, and givings of thanks, be made for all men: for kings and all who are in high places; that we may lead a tranquil and quiet life in all godliness and reverence.

I TIMOTHY 2:1–2 WEB

Since everything God created is good, we should not reject any of it. We may receive it gladly, with thankful hearts. For we know it is made holy by the word of God and prayer.

I TIMOTHY 4:4–5 NLT

Giving thanks to the Father, Who has qualified and made us fit to share the portion which is the inheritance of the saints (God's holy people) in the Light.

COLOSSIANS 1:12 AB

Let us come before him with thanksgiving and extol him with music and song. For the LORD is the great God, the great King above all gods.

PSALM 95:2–3

Oh, give thanks to the LORD, for He is good! For His mercy endures forever.

I CHRONICLES 16:34 NKJV

111

THANKSGIVING

Let's take our place outside with Jesus, no longer pouring out the sacrificial blood of animals but pouring out sacrificial praises from our lips to God in Jesus' name.

HEBREWS 13:15 MSG

Whatever happens, keep thanking God because of Jesus Christ. This is what God wants you to do.

1 THESSALONIANS 5:18 CEV

All you have made will praise you, O LORD; your saints will extol you. They will tell of the glory of your kingdom and speak of your might.

PSALM 145:10–11

For each new morning with its light,
Father, we thank thee,
For rest and shelter of the night,
Father, we thank thee,
For health and food, for love and friends,
For everything thy goodness sends,
Father, in heaven, we thank thee.
—RALPH WALDO EMERSON

A CHRISTLIKE HEART REFLECTS GOD'S . . .
UNDERSTANDING

Above all and before all, do this: Get Wisdom! Write this at the top of your list: Get Understanding!

PROVERBS 4:7 MSG

Wisdom begins with respect for the LORD; those who obey his orders have good understanding. He should be praised forever.

PSALM 111:10 NCV

There is no wisdom or understanding or counsel against the LORD.

PROVERBS 21:30 NKJV

"Listen and come to me. Pay attention to me. Then you will live. I will make a covenant with you that will last forever. I will give you my faithful love. I promised it to David.... My thoughts are not like your thoughts. And your ways are not like my ways," announces the Lord. "The heavens are higher than the earth. And my ways are higher than your ways. My thoughts are higher than your thoughts."

ISAIAH 55:3, 8–9 NIRV

I have more understanding than the elders, for I obey your precepts.

PSALM 119:100

113

UNDERSTANDING

If you reject criticism, you only harm yourself; but if you listen to correction, you grow in understanding.

PROVERBS 15:32 NLT

I have more understanding than all my teachers, for your decrees are my meditation.

PSALM 119:99 NRSV

Counsel in the heart of man is like deep water; but a man of understanding will draw it out.

PROVERBS 20:5 WEB

Through thy precepts I get understanding; therefore I hate every false way.

PSALM 119:104 RSV

The entrance and unfolding of Your words give light; their unfolding gives understanding (discernment and comprehension) to the simple.

PSALM 119:130 AB

How much better it is to get skillful and godly Wisdom than gold! And to get understanding is to be chosen rather than silver.

PROVERBS 16:16 AB

UNDERSTANDING

Good Sense will scout ahead for danger, Insight will keep an eye out for you. They'll keep you from making wrong turns, or following the bad directions.

PROVERBS 2:11–12 MSG

Stop your foolish ways, and you will live; take the road of understanding.

PROVERBS 9:6 NCV

Good understanding gains favor, but the way of the unfaithful is hard.

PROVERBS 13:15 NKJV

Understanding is like a fountain of life to those who have it. But foolish people are punished for the foolish things they do.

PROVERBS 16:22 NIRV

Give me understanding, and I will keep your law and obey it with all my heart.

PSALM 119:34

A wise person is hungry for truth, while the fool feeds on trash.

PROVERBS 15:14 NLT

UNDERSTANDING

Even a fool, when he keeps silent, is counted wise. When he shuts his lips, he is thought to be discerning.

PROVERBS 17:28 WEB

To get wisdom is to love oneself; to keep understanding is to prosper; to keep understanding is to prosper.

PROVERBS 19:8 NRSV

And we know that the Son of God has come, and has given us understanding so that we may know Him who is true; and we are in Him who is true, in His Son Jesus Christ. This is the true God and eternal life.

1 JOHN 5:20 NASB

Give thy servant therefore an understanding mind to govern thy people, that I may discern between good and evil; for who is able to govern this thy great people?

1 KINGS 3:9 RSV

If there is anything hidden from us as disciples today,
it is because we are not in a fit state to understand it.
As soon as we become fit in spiritual character, the
thing is revealed. It is concealed at God's discretion
until the life is developed sufficiently.
—OSWALD CHAMBERS

A CHRISTLIKE HEART REFLECTS GOD'S . . .
VISION

The counsel of [God] stands fast forever, the thoughts of his heart to all generations.

PSALM 33:11 WEB

Surely the Lord God will do nothing without revealing His secret to His servants the prophets.

AMOS 3:7 AB

Then the LORD told me: "I will give you my message in the form of a vision. Write it clearly enough to be read at a glance. At the time I have decided, my words will come true. You can trust what I say about the future. It may take a long time, but keep on waiting—it will happen!"

HABAKKUK 2:2–3 CEV

"Call to Me and I will answer you, and I will tell you great and mighty things, which you do not know."

JEREMIAH 33:3 NASB

I know what I'm doing. I have it all planned out—plans to take care of you, not abandon you, plans to give you the future you hope for.

JEREMIAH 29:11 MSG

VISION

He makes known secrets that are deep and hidden; he knows what is hidden in darkness, and light is all around him.

DANIEL 2:22 NCV

Eye has not seen, nor ear heard, nor have entered into the heart of man the things which God has prepared for those who love Him. But God has revealed them to us through His Spirit. For the Spirit searches all things, yes, the deep things of God.

1 CORINTHIANS 2:9–10 NKJV

He [the prophet Joel] said, "In the last days, God says, I will pour out my Holy Spirit on all people. Your sons and daughters will prophesy. Your young men will see visions. Your old men will have dreams. In those days I will pour out my Spirit even on those who serve me, both men and women. When I do, they will prophesy."

ACTS 2:17–18 NIRV

Waiting upon God is necessary in order to see Him, to have a vision of Him.... Our hearts are like a sensitive photographer's plate; and in order to have God revealed there, we must sit at His feet a long time.

—LETTIE B. COWMAN

A CHRISTLIKE HEART REFLECTS GOD'S . . .
WISDOM

The wise in heart accept commands, but a chattering fool comes to ruin.

PROVERBS 10:8

Don't be impressed with your own wisdom. Instead, fear the LORD and turn your back on evil. Then you will gain renewed health and vitality.

PROVERBS 3:7–8 NLT

By wisdom a house is built, and by understanding it is established; by knowledge the rooms are filled with all precious and pleasant riches.

PROVERBS 24:3–4 NRSV

For I will give you a mouth and wisdom, which none of your adversaries will be able to withstand or contradict.

LUKE 21:15 RSV

Through me, you will live a long time. Years will be added to your life.

PROVERBS 9:11 NIRV

"I, wisdom, dwell with prudence, and I find knowledge and discretion.

PROVERBS 8:12 NASB

WISDOM

That they may know the mystery of God, both of the Father and of Christ in whom are all the treasures of wisdom and knowledge hidden.

COLOSSIANS 2:2–3 WEB

But it is from Him that you have your life in Christ Jesus, Whom God made our Wisdom from God, [revealed to us a knowledge of the divine plan of salvation previously hidden, manifesting itself as] our Righteousness [thus making us upright and putting us in right standing with God], and our Consecration [making us pure and holy], and our Redemption [providing our ransom from eternal penalty for sin].

1 CORINTHIANS 1:30 AB

Don't turn away or become bitter when the LORD corrects you. The LORD corrects everyone he loves, just as parents correct their favorite child.

PROVERBS 3:11–12 CEV

Real wisdom, God's wisdom, begins with a holy life and is characterized by getting along with others. It is gentle and reasonable, overflowing with mercy and blessings, not hot one day and cold the next, not two-faced.

JAMES 3:17 MSG

WISDOM

Only the LORD gives wisdom; he gives knowledge and understanding. He stores up wisdom for those who are honest. Like a shield he protects the innocent.

PROVERBS 2:6–7 NCV

You, through Your commandments, make me wiser than my enemies; for they are ever with me.

PSALM 119:98 NKJV

We have the mind of Christ.

1 CORINTHIANS 2:16

If you need wisdom—if you want to know what God wants you to do—ask him, and he will gladly tell you. He will not resent your asking.

JAMES 1:5 NLT

She [Wisdom] is more precious than jewels, and nothing you desire can compare with her. Long life is in her right hand; in her left hand are riches and honor. Her ways are ways of pleasantness, and all her paths are peace. She is a tree of life to those who lay hold of her; those who hold her fast are called happy.

PROVERBS 3:15–18 NRSV

WISDOM

There is one whose rash words are like sword thrusts, but the tongue of the wise brings healing.

PROVERBS 12:18 RSV

[Grace] which he made to abound toward us in all wisdom and prudence, making known to us the mystery of his will, according to his good pleasure which he purposed in him.

EPHESIANS 1:8–9 WEB

I will bless the Lord, Who has given me counsel; yes, my heart instructs me in the night seasons.

PSALM 16:7 AB

Words of wisdom spoken softly make much more sense than the shouts of a ruler to a crowd of fools.

ECCLESIASTES 9:17 CEV

You have an anointing from the Holy One, and you all know.

1 JOHN 2:20 NASB

What a wildly wonderful world, GOD! You made it all, with Wisdom at your side, made earth overflow with your wonderful creations.

PSALM 104:24 MSG

WISDOM

The LORD made the earth, using his wisdom. He set the sky in place, using his understanding.

PROVERBS 3:19 NCV

Commit your works to the Lord, and your thoughts will be established.

PROVERBS 16:3 NKJV

He will be the firm foundation for their entire lives. He will give them all of the wisdom, knowledge and saving power they will ever need. Respect for the Lord is the key to that treasure.

ISAIAH 33:6 NIRV

I love those who love me, and those who seek me find me.

PROVERBS 8:17

"Anyone who listens to my teaching and obeys me is wise, like a person who builds a house on solid rock."

MATTHEW 7:24 NLT

For God's foolishness is wiser than human wisdom, and God's weakness is stronger than human strength.

1 CORINTHIANS 1:25 NRSV

WISDOM

Happy is the man who finds wisdom, and the man who gets understanding, for the gain from it is better than gain from silver and its profit better than gold.

PROVERBS 3:13–14 RSV

> *May we not ask Him to bring His perfect fore knowledge to bear on all our mental training and storing? To guide us to read or study exactly what He knows there will be use for in the work to which He has called or will call us?*
> —FRANCES RIDLEY HAVERGAL

A CHRISTLIKE HEART REFLECTS GOD'S . . .
ZEAL

The effective, earnest prayer of a righteous man is powerfully effective.

JAMES 5:16 WEB

For the grace of God (His unmerited favor and blessing) has come forward (appeared) for the deliverance from sin and the eternal salvation for all mankind. It has trained us to reject and renounce all ungodliness (irreligion) and worldly (passionate) desires, to live discreet (temperate, self-controlled), upright, devout (spiritually whole) lives in this present world, awaiting and looking for the [fulfillment, the realization of our] blessed hope, even the glorious appearing of our great God and Savior Christ Jesus (the Messiah, the Anointed One), who gave Himself on our behalf that He might redeem us (purchase our freedom) from all iniquity and purify for Himself a people [to be peculiarly His own, people who are] eager and enthusiastic about [living a life that is good and filled with] beneficial deeds.

TITUS 2:11–14 AB

ZEAL

You obeyed the truth, and your souls were made pure. Now you sincerely love each other. But you must keep on loving with all your heart. Do this because God has given you new birth by his message that lives on forever.

1 PETER 1:22–23 CEV

It is good always to be eagerly sought in a commendable manner, and not only when I am present with you.

GALATIANS 4:18 NASB

My zeal wears me out, because my enemies ignore your words. Your promises have been thoroughly tested, and your servant loves them.

PSALM 119:139–140 WEB

Above all things have intense and unfailing love for one another, for love covers [forgives] a multitude of sins.

1 PETER 4:8 AB

Work hard at whatever you do. You will soon go to the world of the dead, where no one works or thinks or reasons or knows anything.

ECCLESIASTES 9:10 CEV

ZEAL

A child will be born to us. A son will be given to us. He will rule over us. And he will be called Wonderful Adviser and Mighty God. He will also be called Father Who Lives Forever and Prince Who Brings Peace. The authority of his rule will continue to grow. The peace he brings will never end. He will rule on David's throne and over his kingdom. He will make the kingdom strong and secure. His rule will be based on what is fair and right. It will last forever. The Lord's great love will make sure that happens. He rules over all.

ISAIAH 9:6–7 NIRV

Brothers, my heart's desire and prayer to God for the Israelites is that they may be saved. For I can testify about them that they are zealous for God, but their zeal is not based on knowledge. Since they did not know the righteousness that comes from God and sought to establish their own, they did not submit to God's righteousness. Christ is the end of the law so that there may be righteousness for everyone who believes.

ROMANS 10:1–4

I am the one who corrects and disciplines everyone I love. Be diligent and turn from your indifference.

REVELATION 3:19 NLT

A CHRISTLIKE HEART REFLECTS GOD'S . . .
ZEAL

Spirit-filled souls are ablaze for God. They love with a love that glows. They believe with a faith that kindles. They serve with a devotion that consumes. They hate sin with a fierceness that burns. They rejoice with a joy that radiates. Love is perfected in the fire of God.
—SAMUEL CHADWICK

A STUDENT RELIES ON GOD REGARDING . . .

THE ONES WHO HAVE TAKEN A STAND, WHO HAVE DRAWN A BOUNDARY-LINE SHARP AND DEEP ABOUT THEIR RELIGIOUS LIFE, WHO HAVE MARKED OFF ALL BEYOND AS FOREVER FORBIDDEN GROUND TO THEM, FIND THE YOKE EASY AND THE BURDEN LIGHT. FOR THIS FORBIDDEN ENVIRONMENT COMES TO BE AS IF IT WERE NOT.... AND THE BALM OF DEATH NUMBING THE LOWER NATURE RELEASES THEM FOR THE SCARCE DISTURBED COMMUNION OF A HIGHER LIFE. SO EVEN HERE TO DIE IS GAIN.

–HENRY DRUMMOND

SINCE WE HAVE SO GREAT A CLOUD OF WITNESSES SURROUNDING US, LET US ALSO LAY ASIDE EVERY ENCUMBRANCE AND THE SIN WHICH SO EASILY ENTANGLES US, AND LET US RUN WITH ENDURANCE THE RACE THAT IS SET BEFORE US.

–HEBREWS 12:1 NASB

ANGER

The wise watch their steps and avoid evil; fools are headstrong and reckless. The hotheaded do things they'll later regret; the coldhearted get the cold shoulder.... Slowness to anger makes for deep understanding; a quick-tempered person stockpiles stupidity.

PROVERBS 14:16–17, 29 MSG

But I say to you, love your enemies. Pray for those who hurt you. If you do this, you will be true children of your Father in heaven. He causes the sun to rise on good people and on evil people, and he sends rain to those who do right and to those who do wrong.

MATTHEW 5:44–45 NCV

So then, my beloved brethren, let every man be swift to hear, slow to speak, slow to wrath; for the wrath of man does not produce the righteousness of God.

JAMES 1:19–20 NKJV

A gentle answer turns anger away. But mean words stir up anger.... A man who burns with anger stirs up fights. But a person who is patient calms things down.

PROVERBS 15:1, 18 NIRV

ANGER

Do all things without complaining and disputing, that you may become blameless and harmless, children of God without fault in the midst of a crooked and perverse generation, among whom you shine as lights in the world.

PHILIPPIANS 2:14–15 NKJV

People with good sense restrain their anger; they earn esteem by overlooking wrongs.

PROVERBS 19:11 NLT

One who is slow to anger is better than the mighty, and one whose temper is controlled than one who captures a city.

PROVERBS 16:32 NRSV

He who despises his neighbor is a sinner, but happy is he who is kind to the poor.

PROVERBS 14:21 RSV

Mockers stir up a city, but wise men turn away anger.

PROVERBS 29:8 WEB

We are part of the same body. Stop lying and start telling each other the truth. Don't get so angry that you sin. Don't go to bed angry.

EPHESIANS 4:25–26 CEV

ANGER

All that the Law says can be summed up in the command to love others as much as you love yourself. But if you keep attacking each other like wild animals, you had better watch out or you will destroy yourselves. If you are guided by the Spirit, you won't obey your selfish desires.

GALATIANS 5:14–16 CEV

But now you also, put them all aside: anger, wrath, malice, slander, and abusive speech from your mouth.

COLOSSIANS 3:8 NASB

Anger is a weed, hate is the tree.
—AUGUSTINE OF HIPPO

A STUDENT RELIES ON GOD REGARDING ... ◆ ◆

ANXIETY

If you wake me each morning with the sound of your loving voice, I'll go to sleep each night trusting in you. Point out the road I must travel; I'm all ears, all eyes before you.... Teach me how to live to please you, because you're my God. Lead me by your blessed Spirit into cleared and level pastureland.

PSALM 143:8, 10 MSG

It is no use for you to get up early and stay up late, working for a living. The LORD gives sleep to those he loves.

PSALM 127:2 NCV

I have walked in my integrity. I have also trusted in the LORD; I shall not slip.

PSALM 26:1 NKJV

Turn all your worries over to him. He cares about you.

1 PETER 5:7 NIRV

When I said, "My foot is slipping," your love, O LORD, supported me.

PSALM 94:18

I keep the LORD always before me; because he is at my right hand, I shall not be moved.

PSALM 16:8 RSV

ANXIETY

Such people will not be overcome by evil circumstances. Those who are righteous will be long remembered. They do not fear bad news; they confidently trust the LORD to care for them.

PSALM 112:6–7 NLT

Wondrously show your steadfast love, O savior of those who seek refuge from their adversaries at your right hand. Guard me as the apple of the eye; hide me in the shadow of your wings.

PSALM 17:7–8 NRSV

Therefore my heart is glad, and my tongue rejoices. My body shall also dwell in safety.

PSALM 16:9 WEB

You have put more joy and rejoicing in my heart than [they know] when their wheat and new wine have yielded abundantly.

PSALM 4:7 AB

God never built a Christian strong enough to carry today's duties and tomorrow's anxieties piled on top of them.
—THEODORE LEDYARD CUYLER

134

A STUDENT RELIES ON GOD REGARDING ... ◆ ◆
ATTITUDE

In your lives you must think and act like Christ Jesus. Christ himself was like God in everything. But he did not think that being equal with God was something to be used for his own benefit.... And when he was living as a man, he humbled himself and was fully obedient to God, even when that caused his death—death on a cross. So God raised him to the highest place. God made his name greater than every other name.

PHILIPPIANS 2:5–6, 8–9 NCV

He said, "That you love the Lord your God with all your passion and prayer and muscle and intelligence—and that you love your neighbor as well as you do yourself." "Good answer!" said Jesus. "Do it and you'll live."

LUKE 10:27–28 MSG

Be renewed in the spirit of your mind, and that you put on the new man which was created according to God, in true righteousness and holiness.

EPHESIANS 4:23–24 NKJV

ATTITUDE

You are God's chosen people. You are holy and dearly loved.
So put on tender mercy and kindness as if they were your
clothes. Don't be proud. Be gentle and patient. Put up with
each other. Forgive the things you are holding against one
another. Forgive, just as the Lord forgave you.

COLOSSIANS 3:12–14 NIRV

Whatever your hand finds to do, do it with all your might,
for in the grave, where you are going, there is neither working nor planning nor knowledge nor wisdom.

ECCLESIASTES 9:10

In everything you do, stay away from complaining and argu-
ing, so that no one can speak a word of blame against you.
You are to live clean, innocent lives as children of God in a
dark world full of crooked and perverse people. Let your lives
shine brightly before them.

PHILIPPIANS 2:14–15 NLT

Therefore prepare your minds for action; discipline yourselves;
set all your hope on the grace that Jesus Christ will bring you
when he is revealed. Like obedient children, do not be conformed to the desires that you formerly had in ignorance.

1 PETER 1:13–16 NRSV

ATTITUDE

Finally, all of you, have unity of spirit, sympathy, love of the brethren, a tender heart and a humble mind. Do not return evil for evil or reviling for reviling; but on the contrary bless, for to this you have been called, that you may obtain a blessing.

I PETER 3:8–9 RSV

"For who has known the mind of the Lord, that he should instruct him?" But we have Christ's mind.

I CORINTHIANS 2:16 WEB

Serve the Lord with gladness! Come before His presence with singing! Know (perceive, recognize, and understand with approval) that the Lord is God! It is He Who has made us, not we ourselves [and we are His]! We are His people and the sheep of His pasture. Enter into His gates with thanksgiving and a thank offering and into His courts with praise! Be thankful and say so to Him, bless and affectionately praise His name! For the Lord is good; His mercy and loving-kindness are everlasting, His faithfulness and truth endure to all generations.

PSALM 100:2–5 AB

ATTITUDE

Always be glad because of the Lord! I will say it again: Be glad. Always be gentle with others. The Lord will soon be here.

PHILIPPIANS 4:4–5 CEV

I call heaven and earth to witness against you today, that I have set before you life and death, the blessing and the curse. So choose life in order that you may live, you and your descendants.

DEUTERONOMY 30:19 NASB

Doubt indulged soon becomes doubt realized.
—FRANCES RIDLEY HAVERGAL

A STUDENT RELIES ON GOD REGARDING ... ◆ ◆
CONFLICT

Our fight is not against human beings. It is against the rulers, the authorities and the powers of this dark world. It is against the spiritual forces of evil in the heavenly world.

EPHESIANS 6:12 NIRV

To this you were called, because Christ suffered for you, leaving you an example, that you should follow in his steps.... When they hurled their insults at him, he did not retaliate; when he suffered, he made no threats. Instead, he entrusted himself to him who judges justly.

I PETER 2:21, 23

In the shelter of your presence you hide them from the intrigues of men; in your dwelling you keep them safe from accusing tongues.

PSALM 31:20

Throw out the mocker, and fighting, quarrels, and insults will disappear.

PROVERBS 22:10 NLT

For lack of wood the fire goes out, and where there is no whisperer, quarreling ceases.

PROVERBS 26:20 NRSV

CONFLICT

A greedy man stirs up strife, but he who trusts in the LORD will be enriched.

PROVERBS 28:25 RSV

Whenever you stand praying, forgive, if you have anything against anyone; so that your Father, who is in heaven, may also forgive you your transgressions. But if you do not forgive, neither will your Father in heaven forgive your transgressions.

MARK 11:25–26 WEB

Finally, brethren, farewell (rejoice)! Be strengthened (perfected, completed, made what you ought to be); be encouraged and consoled and comforted; be of the same [agreeable] mind one with another; live in peace, and [then] the God of love [Who is the Source of affection, goodwill, love, and benevolence toward men] and the Author and Promoter of peace will be with you.

2 CORINTHIANS 13:11 AB

When we please the LORD, even our enemies make friends with us.

PROVERBS 16:7 CEV

CONFLICT

Keeping away from strife is an honor for a man, but any fool will quarrel.

PROVERBS 20:3 NASB

It's the person who loves brother and sister who dwells in God's light and doesn't block the light from others. But whoever hates is still in the dark, stumbles around in the dark, doesn't know which end is up, blinded by the darkness.

I JOHN 2:10–11 MSG

Try to live in peace with all people, and try to live free from sin. Anyone whose life is not holy will never see the Lord.

HEBREWS 12:14 NCV

I will cry out to God Most High, to God who performs all things for me. He shall send from heaven and save me; He reproaches the one who would swallow me up. God shall send forth His mercy and His truth.

PSALM 57:2–3 NKJV

CONFLICT

Would not the carrying out of one single command-
ment of Christ, "Love one another," change the whole
aspect of the world and sweep away prisons and
workhouses, and envying and strife, and all the
strongholds of the devil?
—MAX MULLER

A STUDENT RELIES ON GOD REGARDING ... ◆ ◆
CONFUSION

God is not a God of confusion but of peace, as in all the churches of the saints.

1 CORINTHIANS 14:33 NASB

Let the peace of Christ keep you in tune with each other, in step with each other. None of this going off and doing your own thing. And cultivate thankfulness.

COLOSSIANS 3:15 MSG

Where jealousy and selfishness are, there will be confusion and every kind of evil. But the wisdom that comes from God is first of all pure, then peaceful, gentle, and easy to please. This wisdom is always ready to help those who are troubled and to do good for others. It is always fair and honest.

JAMES 3:16–17 NCV

To him the doorkeeper opens, and the sheep hear his voice; and he calls his own sheep by name and leads them out. And when he brings out his own sheep, he goes before them; and the sheep follow him, for they know his voice. Yet they will by no means follow a stranger, but will flee from him, for they do not know the voice of strangers."

JOHN 10:3–5 NKJV

CONFUSION

"Everyone who is of the truth hears My voice."

JOHN 18:37 NKJV

Your word is like a lamp that shows me the way. It is like a light that guides me.

PSALM 119:105 NIRV

Let me hear of your unfailing love to me in the morning, for I am trusting you. Show me where to walk, for I have come to you in prayer.

PSALM 143:8 NLT

Lead me, O Lord, in your righteousness because of my enemies; make your way straight before me.

PSALM 5:8 NRSV

In thee, O LORD, do I take refuge; let me never be put to shame! In thy righteousness deliver me and rescue me; incline thy ear to me, and save me! Be thou to me a rock of refuge, a strong fortress, to save me, for thou art my rock and my fortress.

PSALM 71:1–3 RSV

CONFUSION

I will bring the blind by a way that they don't know; in paths that they don't know will I lead them; I will make darkness light before them, and crooked places straight. These things will I do, and I will not forsake them.

ISAIAH 42:16 WEB

If any of you need wisdom, you should ask God, and it will be given to you. God is generous and won't correct you for asking. But when you ask for something, you must have faith and not doubt. Anyone who doubts is like an ocean wave tossed around in a storm.... So don't expect the Lord to give you anything at all.

JAMES 1:5–6, 8 CEV

Be still, and know (recognize and understand) that I am God.

PSALM 46:10 AB

Without God, the world would be a maze without a clue.
—WOODROW WILSON

DEPRESSION

The cords of death encompassed me, and the torrents of ungodliness terrified me.... In my distress I called upon the LORD, and cried to my God for help; He heard my voice out of His temple, and my cry for help before Him came into His ears. He sent from on high, He took me; He drew me out of many waters.

PSALM 18:4, 6, 16 NASB

GOD takes the side of the helpless; when I was at the end of my rope, he saved me. I said to myself, "Relax and rest. GOD has showered you with blessings. Soul, you've been rescued from death; Eye, you've been rescued from tears; and you, Foot, were kept from stumbling."

PSALM 116:6–8 MSG

The LORD defends those who suffer; he defends them in times of trouble.

PSALM 9:9 NCV

He delivers the poor in their affliction, and opens their ears in oppression.

JOB 36:15 NKJV

DEPRESSION

How long must I bear pain in my soul, and have sorrow in my heart all day long? How long shall my enemy be exalted over me? Consider and answer me, O Lord my God! Give light to my eyes, or I will sleep the sleep of death.... But I trusted in your steadfast love; my heart shall rejoice in your salvation.

PSALM 13:2–3, 5 NRSV

The LORD gives you relief from suffering and turmoil and cruel bondage.

ISAIAH 14:3

For he satisfies the thirsty and fills the hungry with good things.

PSALM 107:9 NLT

How God anointed Jesus of Nazareth with the Holy Spirit and with power; how he went about doing good and healing all who were oppressed by the devil, for God was with him.

ACTS 10:38 NRSV

I will rejoice and be glad for thy steadfast love, because thou hast seen my affliction, thou hast taken heed of my adversities.

PSALM 31:7 RSV

DEPRESSION

He will fulfill the desire of those who fear him. He also will hear their cry, and will save them. [God] preserves all those who love him, but all the wicked he will destroy.

PSALM 145:19–20 WEB

Lord, You have brought my life up from Sheol (the place of the dead); You have kept me alive, that I should not go down to the pit (the grave).

PSALM 30:3 AB

Your faithful people, LORD, will praise you with songs and honor your holy name.

PSALM 30:4 CEV

Who executes justice for the oppressed; who gives food to the hungry. The LORD sets the prisoners free. The LORD opens the eyes of the blind; the LORD raises up those who are bowed down; the LORD loves the righteous.

PSALM 146:7–8 NASB

My heart is severely pained within me, and the terrors of death have fallen upon me. Fearfulness and trembling have come upon me, and horror has overwhelmed me.... As for me, I will call upon God, and the LORD shall save me.

DEPRESSION

Evening and morning and at noon I will pray, and cry aloud, and He shall hear my voice.

PSALM 55:4–5, 16–17 NKJV

Don't let the floods cover me. Don't let the deep water swallow me up. Don't let the grave close its mouth over me. Lord, answer me because your love is so good. Turn to me because you are so kind. Don't turn your face away from me. Answer me quickly. I'm in trouble.

PSALM 69:15–17 NIRV

Then we cried out to the LORD, the God of our fathers, and the LORD heard our voice and saw our misery, toil and oppression.

DEUTERONOMY 26:7

O God, you are my God; I earnestly search for you. My soul thirsts for you; my whole body longs for you in this parched and weary land where there is no water.... I think how much you have helped me; I sing for joy in the shadow of your protecting wings. I follow close behind you; your strong right hand holds me securely.

PSALM 63:1, 7–8 NLT

DEPRESSION

As a hart longs for flowing streams, so longs my soul for thee, O God. My soul thirsts for God, for the living God. When shall I come and behold the face of God? My tears have been my food day and night, while men say to me continually, "Where is your God?" These things I remember, as I pour out my soul: how I went with the throng, and led them in procession to the house of God, with glad shouts and songs of thanksgiving, a multitude keeping festival.... Deep calls to deep at the thunder of thy cataracts; all thy waves and thy billows have gone over me. By day the LORD commands his steadfast love; and at night his song is with me, a prayer to the God of my life.

PSALM 42:1–4, 7–8 RSV

For my iniquities have gone over my head. As a heavy burden, they are too heavy for me.... I am pained and bowed down greatly. I go mourning all day long.... My heart throbs. My strength fails me. As for the light of my eyes, it also is gone from me.... For in you, [Lord], do I hope. You will answer, Lord my God.... Don't forsake me, [Lord]. My God, don't be far from me. Hurry to help me, Lord, my salvation.

PSALM 38:4, 6, 10, 15, 21–22 WEB

DEPRESSION

Because of and through the heart of tender mercy and loving-kindness of our God, a Light from on high will dawn upon us and visit [us] to shine upon and give light to those who sit in darkness and in the shadow of death, to direct and guide our feet in a straight line into the way of peace.

LUKE 1:78–79 AB

Lead, kindly Light, amid th' encircling gloom;
Lead thou me on.
The night is dark, and I am far from home;
Lead thou me on.
Keep thou my feet; I do not ask to see
The distance scene—one step enough for me.
—CARDINAL JOHN HENRY NEWMAN

DISCOURAGEMENT

You let me rest in fields of green grass. You lead me to streams of peaceful water, and you refresh my life. You are true to your name, and you lead me along the right paths.

PSALM 23:2–3 CEV

"Now it's time to change your ways! Turn to face God so he can wipe away your sins, pour out showers of blessing to refresh you."

ACTS 3:19 MSG

We must not become tired of doing good. We will receive our harvest of eternal life at the right time if we do not give up.

GALATIANS 6:9 NCV

If you extend your soul to the hungry and satisfy the afflicted soul, then your light shall dawn in the darkness, and your darkness shall be as the noonday. The LORD will guide you continually, and satisfy your soul in drought, and strengthen your bones; You shall be like a watered garden, and like a spring of water, whose waters do not fail.

ISAIAH 58:10–11 NKJV

Write down my poem of sadness. List my tears on your scroll. Aren't you making a record of them?

PSALM 56:8 NIRV

DISCOURAGEMENT

They mounted up to the heavens and went down to the depths; in their peril their courage melted away. They reeled and staggered like drunken men; they were at their wits' end. Then they cried out to the LORD in their trouble, and he brought them out of their distress. He stilled the storm to a whisper; the waves of the sea were hushed. They were glad when it grew calm, and he guided them to their desired haven.

PSALM 107:26–30

My flesh and my heart may fail, but God is the strength of my heart and my portion for ever.

PSALM 73:26 RSV

GOD is good to one and all; everything he does is suffused with grace.

PSALM 145:9 MSG

Cruel strangers have attacked and want me dead. Not one of them cares about you. You will help me, Lord God, and keep me from falling.

PSALM 54:3–4 CEV

DISCOURAGEMENT

Because he has set his love on me, therefore I will deliver him. I will set him on high, because he has known my name. He will call on me, and I will answer him. I will be with him in trouble. I will deliver him, and honor him.

PSALM 91:14–15 WEB

The hope of the [uncompromisingly] righteous (the upright, in right standing with God) is gladness, but the expectation of the wicked (those who are out of harmony with God) comes to nothing.

PROVERBS 10:28 AB

We pray that you'll have the strength to stick it out over the long haul—not the grim strength of gritting your teeth but the glory-strength God gives. It is strength that endures the unendurable and spills over into joy.

COLOSSIANS 1:11 MSG

DISCOURAGEMENT

Then I said, "It is my grief, that the right hand of the Most High has changed." I shall remember the deeds of the LORD; surely I will remember Your wonders of old. I will meditate on all Your work and muse on Your deeds. Your way, O God, is holy; what god is great like our God? You are the God who works wonders; You have made known Your strength among the peoples.

PSALM 77:10–14 NASB

Answer me when I pray to you, my God who does what is right. Make things easier for me when I am in trouble. Have mercy on me and hear my prayer.

PSALM 4:1 NCV

Happy is he who has the God of Jacob for his help, whose hope is in the LORD his God.

PSALM 146:5 NKJV

Lord, you have deep concern for me. Keep me alive as you have promised.

PSALM 119:156 NIRV

DISCOURAGEMENT

Whom have I in heaven but you? And earth has nothing I desire besides you.... But as for me, it is good to be near God. I have made the Sovereign LORD my refuge; I will tell of all your deeds.

PSALM 73:25, 28

"Not even a sparrow, worth only half a penny, can fall to the ground without your Father knowing it. And the very hairs on your head are all numbered."

MATTHEW 10:29–30 NLT

I lie down and sleep; I wake again, for the Lord sustains me.

PSALM 3:5 NRSV

Hope deferred makes the heart sick, but a desire fulfilled is a tree of life.

PROVERBS 13:12 RSV

Also delight yourself in [the Lord], and he will give you the desires of your heart.

PSALM 37:4 WEB

DISCOURAGEMENT

For He has not despised or abhorred the affliction of the afflicted; neither has He hidden His face from him, but when he cried to Him, He heard. My praise shall be of You in the great congregation. I will pay to Him my vows [made in the time of trouble] before them who fear (revere and worship) Him.

PSALM 22:24–25 AB

Who may climb the LORD's hill or stand in his holy temple? Only those who do right for the right reasons, and don't worship idols or tell lies under oath. The LORD God, who saves them, will bless and reward them.

PSALM 24:3–5 CEV

When we yield to discouragement, it is usually because we give too much thought to the past or to the future.
—THERESE OF LISIEUX

157

DOUBT

The point is, before you trust, you have to listen. But unless Christ's Word is preached, there's nothing to listen to.

ROMANS 10:17 MSG

And this is the boldness we have in God's presence: that if we ask God for anything that agrees with what he wants, he hears us.

1 JOHN 5:14 NCV

Therefore I say to you, whatever things you ask when you pray, believe that you receive them, and you will have them.

MARK 11:24 NKJV

On the way, they had argued about which one of them was the most important person. Jesus sat down and called for the Twelve to come to him. Then he said, "If you want to be first, you must be the very last. You must be the servant of everyone."

MARK 9:34–35 NIRV

These are written that you may believe that Jesus is the Christ, the Son of God, and that believing you may have life in his name.

JOHN 20:31 RSV

DOUBT

Early in the morning they left for the Desert of Tekoa. As they set out, Jehoshaphat stood and said, "Listen to me, Judah and people of Jerusalem! Have faith in the LORD your God and you will be upheld; have faith in his prophets and you will be successful."

2 CHRONICLES 20:20

I write this to you who believe in the Son of God, so that you may know you have eternal life.

1 JOHN 5:13 NLT

Only it must be in faith that he asks with no wavering (no hesitating, no doubting). For the one who wavers (hesitates, doubts) is like the billowing surge out at sea that is blown hither and thither and tossed by the wind. For truly, let not such a person imagine that he will receive anything [he asks for] from the Lord, [for being as he is] a man of two minds (hesitating, dubious, irresolute), [he is] unstable and unreliable and uncertain about everything [he thinks, feels, decides].

JAMES 1:6–8 AB

DOUBT

In times of dryness and desolation we must be patient, and wait with resignation the return of consolation, putting our trust in the goodness of God. We must animate ourselves by the thought that God is always with us, that He only allows this trial for our greater good, and that we have not necessarily lost His grace because we have lost the taste of feeling it.

—IGNATIUS OF LOYALA

A STUDENT RELIES ON GOD REGARDING ... ◆ ◆
FEAR

You will not be harmed, though thousands fall all around you. And with your own eyes you will see the punishment of the wicked. The LORD Most High is your fortress. Run to him for safety, and no terrible disasters will strike you or your home.

PSALM 91:7–10 CEV

Be strong and let your heart take courage, all you who hope in the LORD.

PSALM 31:24 NASB

You are my hiding place and my shield; I wait for Your word.... Uphold me that I may be safe, that I may have regard for Your statutes continually.

PSALM 119:114, 117 NASB

It is no use for you to get up early and stay up late, working for a living. The LORD gives sleep to those he loves.

PSALM 127:2 NCV

Such love has no fear because perfect love expels all fear. If we are afraid, it is for fear of judgment, and this shows that his love has not been perfected in us.

1 JOHN 4:18 NLT

FEAR

Thus says the LORD, who created you ... and He who formed you, O Israel: "Fear not, for I have redeemed you; I have called you by your name; you are Mine."

ISAIAH 43:1 NKJV

Turn your worries over to the Lord. He will keep you going. He will never let godly people fall.

PSALM 55:22 NIRV

Peace I leave with you; my peace I give you. I do not give to you as the world gives. Do not let your hearts be troubled and do not be afraid.

JOHN 14:27

I prayed to the LORD, and he answered me, freeing me from all my fears.

PSALM 34:4 NLT

No weapon that is fashioned against you shall prosper, and you shall confute every tongue that rises against you in judgment. This is the heritage of the servants of the Lord and their vindication from me, says the Lord.

ISAIAH 54:17 NRSV

FEAR

Fear not, for I am with you, be not dismayed, for I am your God; I will strengthen you, I will help you, I will uphold you with my victorious right hand.

ISAIAH 41:10 RSV

For you didn't receive the spirit of bondage again to fear, but you received the spirit of adoption, whereby we cry, "Abba! Father!"

ROMANS 8:15 WEB

Yes, though I walk through the [deep, sunless] valley of the shadow of death, I will fear or dread no evil, for You are with me; Your rod [to protect] and Your staff [to guide], they comfort me.

PSALM 23:4 AB

You, LORD, are the light that keeps me safe. I am not afraid of anyone. You protect me, and I have no fears.... Armies may surround me, but I won't be afraid; war may break out, but I will trust you.

PSALM 27:1, 3 CEV

"For I, the LORD, do not change; therefore you ... are not consumed."

MALACHI 3:6 NASB

FEAR

Into the hovels of the poor, into the dark streets where the homeless groan, God speaks: "I've had enough; I'm on my way to heal the ache in the heart of the wretched."

PSALM 12:5 MSG

The wise man in the storm prays to God, not for safety from danger, but for deliverance from fear. It is the storm within which endangers him, not the storm without.
—RALPH WALDO EMERSON

A STUDENT RELIES ON GOD REGARDING . . . ◆ ◆
FINANCES

Steep your life in God-reality, God-initiative, God-provisions. Don't worry about missing out. You'll find all your everyday human concerns will be met.

MATTHEW 6:33 MSG

Honor the LORD with your wealth and the firstfruits from all your crops. Then your barns will be full, and your wine barrels will overflow with new wine.

PROVERBS 3:9–10 NCV

He who did not spare His own Son, but delivered Him up for us all, how shall He not with Him also freely give us all things?

ROMANS 8:32 NKJV

You know the grace shown by our Lord Jesus Christ. Even though he was rich, he became poor to help you. Because he became poor, you can become rich.

2 CORINTHIANS 8:9 NIRV

With me are riches and honor, enduring wealth and prosperity.... Bestowing wealth on those who love me and making their treasuries full.

PROVERBS 8:18, 21

FINANCES

Oh, the joys of those who do not follow the advice of the wicked, or stand around with sinners, or join in with scoffers. But they delight in doing everything the LORD wants; day and night they think about his law. They are like trees planted along the riverbank, bearing fruit each season without fail. Their leaves never wither, and in all they do, they prosper.

PSALM 1:1–3 NLT

Give, and it will be given to you. A good measure, pressed down, shaken together, running over, will be put into your lap; for the measure you give will be the measure you get back.

LUKE 6:38 NRSV

A slack hand causes poverty, but the hand of the diligent makes rich.

PROVERBS 10:4 RSV

The house of the wicked will be overthrown, but the tent of the upright will flourish.

PROVERBS 14:11 WEB

FINANCES

As for the rich in this world, charge them not to be proud and arrogant and contemptuous of others, nor to set their hopes on uncertain riches, but on God, Who richly and ceaselessly provides us with everything for [our] enjoyment.

I TIMOTHY 6:17 AB

I am poor and needy, but, LORD God, you care about me, and you come to my rescue. Please hurry and help.

PSALM 40:17 CEV

And He said to His disciples, "For this reason I say to you, do not worry about your life, as to what you will eat; nor for your body, as to what you will put on.... But seek His kingdom, and these things will be added to you. Do not be afraid, little flock, for your Father has chosen gladly to give you the kingdom."

LUKE 12:22, 31–32 NASB

Generous hands are blessed hands because they give bread to the poor.

PROVERBS 22:9 MSG

Trust the LORD and do good. Live in the land and feed on truth.

PSALM 37:3 NCV

167

FINANCES

Let them shout for joy and be glad, who favor my righteous cause; and let them say continually, "Let the Lord be magnified, who has pleasure in the prosperity of His servant."

PSALM 35:27 NKJV

The houses of those who do what is right hold great wealth. But those who do what is wrong earn only trouble.

PROVERBS 15:6 NIRV

When they are given over to those who shall condemn them, then they shall learn that my words were pleasant.

PSALM 141:6 NRSV

"Bring the entire tenth to the storerooms in my temple. Then there will be plenty of food. Put me to the test," says the Lord. "Then you will see that I will throw open the windows of heaven. I will pour out so many blessings that you will not have enough room for them."

MALACHI 3:10 NIRV

As long as I can remember, good people have never been left helpless, and their children have never gone begging for food.

PSALM 37:25 CEV

FINANCES

◆ ◆

Whoever trusts in his riches will fall, but the righteous will thrive like a green leaf.

PROVERBS 11:28

Dear friend, I am praying that all is well with you and that your body is as healthy as I know your soul is.

3 JOHN v. 2 NLT

The blessing of the LORD makes rich, and he adds no sorrow with it.

PROVERBS 10:22 RSV

The young lions do lack, and suffer hunger, but those who seek [the Lord] shall not lack any good thing.

PSALM 34:10 WEB

Praise the LORD! How blessed is the man who fears the LORD, who greatly delights in His commandments.... Wealth and riches are in his house, and his righteousness endures forever.

PSALM 112:1, 3 NASB

And my God will liberally supply (fill to the full) your every need according to His riches in glory in Christ Jesus.

PHILIPPIANS 4:19 AB

FINANCES

Remember this—a farmer who plants only a few seeds will get a small crop. But the one who plants generously will get a generous crop. You must each make up your own mind as to how much you should give. Don't give reluctantly or in response to pressure. For God loves the person who gives cheerfully. And God will generously provide all you need. Then you will always have everything you need and plenty left over to share with others.

2 CORINTHIANS 9:6–8 NLT

The eyes of all look to you, and you give them their food at the proper time. You open your hand and satisfy the desires of every living thing.

PSALM 145:15–16

A gracious woman gets honor, but she who hates virtue is covered with shame. The timid become destitute, but the aggressive gain riches.

PROVERBS 11:16 NRSV

Whoever causes the upright to go astray in an evil way, he will fall into his own trap; but the blameless will inherit good.

PROVERBS 28:10 WEB

*There is no portion of our time that is our time, and
the rest God's; there is no portion of money that is
our money, and the rest God's money. It is all His;
He made it all, gives it all, and He has simply trusted it to us for His service. A servant has two purses,
the mater's and his own, but we have only one.*
—ADOLPHE MONOD

A STUDENT RELIES ON GOD REGARDING . . .
GREED

If we have food and clothing, with these we shall be content. But those who desire to be rich fall into temptation, into a snare, into many senseless and hurtful desires that plunge men into ruin and destruction. For the love of money is the root of all evils; it is through this craving that some have wandered away from the faith and pierced their hearts with many pangs. But as for you, man of God, shun all this; aim at righteousness, godliness, faith, love, steadfastness, gentleness.

I TIMOTHY 6:8–11 RSV

All day long the wicked covet, but the righteous give and do not hold back.

PROVERBS 21:26 NRSV

Dishonest money brings grief to the whole family, but those who hate bribes will live.

PROVERBS 15:27 NLT

Death and Destruction are never satisfied, and neither are the eyes of man.

PROVERBS 27:20

GREED

Don't be controlled by love for money. Be happy with what you have. God has said, "I will never leave you. I will never desert you."

HEBREWS 13:5 NIRV

Now godliness with contentment is great gain. For we brought nothing into this world, and it is certain we can carry nothing out.

1 TIMOTHY 6:6–7 NKJV

But they start worrying about the needs of this life. They are fooled by the desire to get rich and to have all kinds of other things. So the message gets choked out, and they never produce anything. The seeds that fell on good ground are the people who hear and welcome the message. They produce thirty or sixty or even a hundred times as much as was planted.

MARK 4:19–20 CEV

Actually, I don't have a sense of needing anything personally. I've learned by now to be quite content whatever my circumstances. I'm just as happy with little as with much, with much as with little. I've found the recipe for being happy whether full or hungry, hands full or hands empty.

PHILIPPIANS 4:11–13 MSG

GREED

The covetous man pines in plenty, like Tantalus up to the chin in water, and yet thirsty.

—THOMAS ADAMS

A STUDENT RELIES ON GOD REGARDING ...
GRIEF

He was despised and rejected and forsaken by men, a Man of sorrows and pains, and acquainted with grief and sickness; and like One from Whom men hide their faces He was despised, and we did not appreciate His worth or have any esteem for Him. Surely He has borne our griefs (sicknesses, weaknesses, and distresses) and carried our sorrows and pains [of punishment], yet we [ignorantly] considered Him stricken, smitten, and afflicted by God [as if with leprosy].

ISAIAH 53:3–4 AB

The Spirit of the Lord is on me; because [the Lord] has anointed me to preach good news to the humble; he has sent me to bind up the broken-hearted, to proclaim liberty to the captives, and the opening [of the prison] to those who are bound; to proclaim the year of [the Lord]'s favor, and the day of vengeance of our God; to comfort all who mourn; to appoint to those who mourn in Zion, to give to them a garland for ashes, the oil of joy for mourning, the garment of praise for the spirit of heaviness; that they may be called trees of righteousness, the planting of [the Lord], that he may be glorified.

ISAIAH 61:1–3 WEB

GRIEF

He renews our hopes and heals our bodies.

PSALM 147:3 CEV

And the ransomed of the LORD will return and come with joyful shouting to Zion, With everlasting joy upon their heads. They will find gladness and joy, and sorrow and sighing will flee away.

ISAIAH 35:10 NASB

GOD's loyal love couldn't have run out, his merciful love couldn't have dried up. They're created new every morning. How great your faithfulness!

LAMENTATIONS 3:22–23 MSG

My eyes are weak from so much crying; they are weak from crying about my enemies. Get away from me, all you who do evil, because the LORD has heard my crying. The LORD has heard my cry for help; the LORD will answer my prayer.

PSALM 6:7–9 NCV

A bruised reed He will not break, and smoking flax He will not quench; He will bring forth justice for truth.

ISAIAH 42:3 NKJV

GRIEF

Blessed are those who are sad. They will be comforted.

MATTHEW 5:4 NIRV

Now may our Lord Jesus Christ himself, and God our Father, who loved us and gave us eternal comfort and good hope through grace, comfort your hearts and establish them in every good work and word.

2 THESSALONIANS 2:16–17 RSV

May those who sow in tears reap with shouts of joy.

PSALM 126:5 NRSV

Those who have been ransomed by the LORD will return to Jerusalem, singing songs of everlasting joy. Sorrow and mourning will disappear, and they will be overcome with joy and gladness. "I, even I, am the one who comforts you. So why are you afraid of mere humans, who wither like the grass and disappear?

ISAIAH 51:11–12 NLT

The LORD will surely comfort Zion and will look with compassion on all her ruins; he will make her deserts like Eden, her wastelands like the garden of the LORD. Joy and gladness will be found in her, thanksgiving and the sound of singing.

ISAIAH 51:3

GRIEF

He has swallowed up death forever; and the Lord will wipe away tears from off all faces; and the reproach of his people will he take away from off all the earth: for [God] has spoken it.

ISAIAH 25:8 WEB

Sing for joy, O heavens, and be joyful, O earth, and break forth into singing, O mountains! For the Lord has comforted His people and will have compassion upon His afflicted. Behold, I have indelibly imprinted (tattooed a picture of) you on the palm of each of My hands; [O Zion] your walls are continually before Me.

ISAIAH 49:13, 16 AB

Have pity, LORD! Help! You have turned my sorrow into joyful dancing. No longer am I sad and wearing sackcloth.

PSALM 30:10–11 CEV

I saw the holy city, new Jerusalem, coming down out of heaven from God, made ready as a bride adorned for her husband. He will wipe away every tear from their eyes; and there will no longer be any death; there will no longer be any mourning, or crying, or pain; the first things have passed away.

REVELATION 21:2, 4 NASB

GRIEF

I am praying to you because I know you will answer, O God. Bend down and listen as I pray. Show me your unfailing love in wonderful ways. By your mighty power you rescue those who seek refuge from their enemies. Guard me as you would guard your own eyes.

Hide me in the shadow of your wings. Protect me from wicked people who attack me, from murderous enemies who surround me.... Rescue me from the wicked with your sword! By the power of your hand, O Lord, destroy those who look to this world for their reward. But satisfy the hunger of your treasured ones. May their children have plenty, leaving an inheritance for their descendants. Because I am righteous, I will see you. When I awake, I will see you face to face and be satisfied.

PSALM 17:6–9, 13–15 NLT

Praise be to the God and Father of our Lord Jesus Christ, the Father of compassion and the God of all comfort, who comforts us in all our troubles, so that we can comfort those in any trouble with the comfort we ourselves have received from God.

2 CORINTHIANS 1:3–4

It is in dying that we are born to eternal life.
—ST. FRANCIS OF ASSISI

A STUDENT RELIES ON GOD REGARDING ... ◆ ◆
ILLNESS

Those who live in the shelter of the Most High will find rest in the shadow of the Almighty.... No evil will conquer you; no plague will come near your dwelling.

PSALM 91:1, 10 NLT

The Lord opens the eyes of the blind. The Lord lifts up those who are bowed down; the Lord loves the righteous.

PSALM 146:8 NRSV

Fools are afflicted because of their disobedience, and because of their iniquities.... He sends his word, and heals them, and delivers them from their graves.

PSALM 107:17, 20 WEB

Heal me, O Lord, and I shall be healed; save me, and I shall be saved, for You are my praise.

JEREMIAH 17:14 AB

Is any among you sick? Let him call for the elders of the church, and let them pray over him, anointing him with oil in the name of the Lord; and the prayer of faith will save the sick man, and the Lord will raise him up; and if he has committed sins, he will be forgiven.

JAMES 5:14–15 RSV

ILLNESS

My child, listen carefully to everything I say. Don't forget a single word, but think about it all. Knowing these teachings will mean true life and good health for you.

PROVERBS 4:20–22 CEV

And He Himself bore our sins in His body on the cross, so that we might die to sin and live to righteousness; for by His wounds you were healed.

1 PETER 2:24 NASB

"If you'll hold on to me for dear life," says GOD, "I'll get you out of any trouble. I'll give you the best of care if you'll only get to know and trust me.... I'll give you a long life, give you a long drink of salvation!"

PSALM 91:14, 16 MSG

Even if I walk through a very dark valley, I will not be afraid, because you are with me. Your rod and your walking stick comfort me.

PSALM 23:4 NCV

Bless the LORD, O my soul, and forget not all His benefits: who forgives all your iniquities, who heals all your diseases.

PSALM 103:2–3 NKJV

182

ILLNESS

My spirit, why are you so sad? Why are you so upset deep down inside me? Put your hope in God. Once again I will have reason to praise him. He is my Savior and my God.

PSALM 43:5 NIRV

He said, "If you listen carefully to the voice of the LORD your God and do what is right in his eyes, if you pay attention to his commands and keep all his decrees, I will not bring on you any of the diseases I brought on the Egyptians, for I am the LORD, who heals you."

EXODUS 15:26

He was wounded for our transgressions, he was bruised for our iniquities; upon him was the chastisement that made us whole, and with his stripes we are healed.

ISAIAH 53:5 RSV

The LORD protects those of childlike faith; I was facing death, and then he saved me.... And so I walk in the LORD's presence as I live here on earth!

PSALM 116:6, 9 NLT

ILLNESS

For you who revere my name the sun of righteousness shall rise, with healing in its wings. You shall go out leaping like calves from the stall.

MALACHI 4:2 NRSV

You, LORD God, bless everyone who cares for the poor, and you rescue those people in times of trouble. You protect them and keep them alive. You make them happy here in this land, and you don't hand them over to their enemies. You always heal them and restore their strength when they are sick.

PSALM 41:1–3 CEV

The life of the body is a heart at peace, but envy rots the bones.

PROVERBS 14:30 WEB

You shall serve the Lord your God; He shall bless your bread and water, and I will take sickness from your midst. None shall lose her young by miscarriage or be barren in your land; I will fulfill the number of your days.

EXODUS 23:25–26 AB

ILLNESS

You know of Jesus of Nazareth, how God anointed Him with the Holy Spirit and with power, and how He went about doing good and healing all who were oppressed by the devil, for God was with Him.

ACTS 10:38 NASB

He is a path, if any be misled;
He is a robe, if any naked be;
If any chance to hunger, He is bread;
If any be a bondman, He is free;
If any be but weak, how strong is He!
To dead men, life is He; to sick men, health;
To blind men, sight; and to the needy, wealth;
A pleasure without loss; a treasure without stealth.
—GILES FLETCHER

IMPURE THOUGHTS

For as he thinks in his heart, so is he. As one who reckons, he says to you, eat and drink, yet his heart is not with you [but is grudging the cost].

PROVERBS 23:7 AB

The world is unprincipled. It's dog-eat-dog out there! The world doesn't fight fair. But we don't live or fight our battles that way—never have and never will. The tools of our trade aren't for marketing or manipulation, but they are for demolishing that entire massively corrupt culture. We use our powerful God-tools for smashing warped philosophies, tearing down barriers erected against the truth of God, fitting every loose thought and emotion and impulse into the structure of life shaped by Christ.

2 CORINTHIANS 10:3–5 MSG

IMPURE THOUGHTS

So brothers and sisters, since God has shown us great mercy, I beg you to offer your lives as a living sacrifice to him. Your offering must be only for God and pleasing to him, which is the spiritual way for you to worship. Do not change yourselves to be like the people of this world, but be changed within by a new way of thinking. Then you will be able to decide what God wants for you; you will know what is good and pleasing to him and what is perfect.

ROMANS 12:1–2 NCV

Wash me thoroughly from my iniquity, and cleanse me from my sin. For I acknowledge my transgressions, and my sin is always before me. Against You, You only, have I sinned, and done this evil in Your sight—that You may be found just when You speak, and blameless when You judge.

PSALM 51:2–4 NKJV

Finally, my brothers and sisters, always think about what is true. Think about what is noble, right and pure. Think about what is lovely and worthy of respect. If anything is excellent or worthy of praise, think about those kinds of things. Do what you have learned or received or heard from me. Follow my example. The God who gives peace will be with you.

PHILIPPIANS 4:8–9 NIRV

IMPURE THOUGHTS

The law of the LORD is perfect, reviving the soul. The statutes of the LORD are trustworthy, making wise the simple.... The fear of the LORD is pure, enduring forever. The ordinances of the LORD are sure and altogether righteous.

PSALM 19:7, 9

How can a young person stay pure? By obeying your word and following its rules.... I have hidden your word in my heart, that I might not sin against you.

PSALM 119:9, 11 NLT

God is faithful and fair. If we admit that we have sinned, he will forgive us our sins. He will forgive every wrong thing we have done. He will make us pure.

1 JOHN 1:9 NIRV

I love your law. You are my hiding place and my shield; I hope in your word. Go away from me, you evildoers, that I may keep the commandments of my God. Uphold me according to your promise, that I may live, and let me not be put to shame in my hope. Hold me up, that I may be safe and have regard for your statutes continually.

PSALM 119:113–117 NRSV

IMPURE THOUGHTS

Who can discern his errors? Forgive me from hidden errors. Keep back your servant also from presumptuous sins. Let them not have dominion over me. Then I will be upright, I will be blameless and innocent of great transgression. Let the words of my mouth and the meditation of my heart be acceptable in your sight, [Lord], my rock, and my redeemer.

PSALM 19:12–14 WEB

A person's mind is the Holy of Holies, and to admit evil thoughts is like setting up an idol in the temple.

—THE BERDICHEVER RABBI

INJUSTICE

Great peace have they who love Your law; nothing shall offend them or make them stumble.

PSALM 119:165 AB

God will bless you, even if others treat you unfairly for being loyal to him. You don't gain anything by being punished for some wrong you have done. But God will bless you, if you have to suffer for doing something good.

1 PETER 2:19–20 CEV

If the world hates you, you know that it has hated Me before it hated you. If you were of the world, the world would love its own; but because you are not of the world, but I chose you out of the world, because of this the world hates you.

JOHN 15:18–19 NASB

GOD makes everything come out right; he puts victims back on their feet.

PSALM 103:6 MSG

Evil people will be sent away, but those who trust the LORD will inherit the land.

PSALM 37:9 NCV

INJUSTICE

You prepare a table before me in the presence of my enemies; You anoint my head with oil; my cup runs over. Surely goodness and mercy shall follow me all the days of my life; and I will dwell in the house of the LORD forever.

PSALM 23:5–6 NKJV

Don't pay back evil with evil. Don't pay back unkind words with unkind words. Instead, pay them back with kind words. That's what you have been chosen to do. You can receive a blessing by doing it. Scripture says, "Do you want to love life and see good days? Then keep your tongues from speaking evil. Keep your lips from telling lies. Turn away from evil, and do good. Look for peace, and go after it."

I PETER 3:9–11 NIRV

For God will bring every deed into judgment, including every hidden thing, whether it is good or evil.

ECCLESIASTES 12:14

"God blesses you when you are mocked and persecuted and lied about because you are my followers. Be happy about it! Be very glad! For a great reward awaits you in heaven. And remember, the ancient prophets were persecuted, too."

MATTHEW 5:11–12 NLT

INJUSTICE

More in number than the hairs of my head are those who hate me without cause; many are those who would destroy me, my enemies who accuse me falsely.... For the Lord hears the needy, and does not despise his own that are in bonds. Let heaven and earth praise him, the seas and everything that moves in them. For God will save Zion and rebuild the cities of Judah; and his servants shall live there and possess it; the children of his servants shall inherit it, and those who love his name shall live in it.

PSALM 69:4, 33–36 NRSV

Who shall bring any charge against God's elect? It is God who justifies; who is to condemn? Is it Christ Jesus, who died, yes, who was raised from the dead, who is at the right hand of God, who indeed intercedes for us?

ROMANS 8:33–34 RSV

I will deliver you in that day, says [the Lord]; and you shall not be given into the hand of the men of whom you are afraid. For I will surely save you, and you shall not fall by the sword, but your life shall be for a prey to you; because you have put your trust in me, says [the Lord].

JEREMIAH 39:17–18 WEB

INJUSTICE

Behold, all they who are enraged and inflamed against you shall be put to shame and confounded; they who strive against you shall be as nothing and shall perish. You shall seek those who contend with you but shall not find them; they who war against you shall be as nothing, as nothing at all. For I the Lord your God hold your right hand; I am the Lord, Who says to you, Fear not; I will help you!

ISAIAH 41:11–13 AB

I will not be afraid of ten thousands of people who have set themselves against me round about. Arise, O LORD; save me, O my God! For You have smitten all my enemies on the cheek; You have shattered the teeth of the wicked. Salvation belongs to the LORD; Your blessing be upon Your people!

PSALM 3:6–8 NASB

Won't God protect his chosen ones who pray to him day and night? Won't he be concerned for them? He will surely hurry and help them. But when the Son of Man comes, will he find on this earth anyone with faith?

LUKE 18:7–8 CEV

INJUSTICE

During danger he will keep me safe in his shelter. He will hide me in his Holy Tent, or he will keep me safe on a high mountain. My head is higher than my enemies around me. I will offer joyful sacrifices in his Holy Tent. I will sing and praise the LORD.

PSALM 27:5–6 NCV

Flee a thousand leagues from saying, "I was in the right. It was not right for me to suffer this. They had no right to treat me so." God deliver us from all such rights. And when we receive honors, or affection, or kind treatment, let us ask what right we have to them.

—SAINT TERESA OF AVILA

A STUDENT RELIES ON GOD REGARDING ...
JEALOUSY

The fear of the Lord is life indeed; filled with it one rests secure and suffers no harm.

PROVERBS 19:23 NRSV

You gain a lot when you live a godly life. But you must be happy with what you have. We didn't bring anything into the world. We can't take anything out of it.

1 TIMOTHY 6:6–7 NIRV

"I'll make sure that their priests get three square meals a day and that my people have more than enough." GOD's Decree.

JEREMIAH 31:14 MSG

Keep your lives free from the love of money, and be satisfied with what you have. God has said, "I will never leave you; I will never forget you."

HEBREWS 13:5 NCV

Let not thine heart envy sinners: but be thou in the fear of the LORD all the day long. For surely there is an end; and thine expectation shall not be cut off.

PROVERBS 23:17–18 KJV

JEALOUSY

[The Lord] satisfies your desires with good things so that your youth is renewed like the eagle's.

PSALM 103:5

One hand full of rest is better than two fists full of labor and striving after wind.

ECCLESIASTES 4:6 NASB

Your unfailing love is better to me than life itself; how I praise you! I will honor you as long as I live, lifting up my hands to you in prayer. You satisfy me more than the richest of foods. I will praise you with songs of joy.

PSALM 63:3–5 NLT

Be still before the LORD, and wait patiently for him; fret not yourself over him who prospers in his way, over the man who carries out evil devices! For the wicked shall be cut off; but those who wait for the LORD shall possess the land.

PSALM 37:7, 9 RSV

Those who belong to Christ have crucified the flesh with its passions and lusts. If we live by the Spirit, let's also walk by the Spirit. Let's not become conceited, provoking one another, and envying one another.

GALATIANS 5:24–26 WEB

JEALOUSY

Do not resentfully envy and be jealous of an unscrupulous, grasping man, and choose none of his ways. For the perverse are an abomination [extremely disgusting and detestable] to the Lord; but His confidential communion and secret counsel are with the [uncompromisingly] righteous (those who are upright and in right standing with Him).

PROVERBS 3:31–32 AB

But if your heart is full of bitter jealousy and selfishness, don't brag or lie to cover up the truth. That kind of wisdom doesn't come from above. It is earthly and selfish and comes from the devil himself.

JAMES 3:14–15 CEV

Love is not jealous or boastful or proud.

I CORINTHIANS 13:4 NLT

A sound heart is life to the body, but envy is rottenness to the bones.

PROVERBS 14:30 NKJV

The jealous are troublesome to others, a torment to themselves.
—WILLIAM PENN

LONELINESS

I want you to realize that the Lord is God. He made us, and we belong to him. We are his people. We are the sheep belonging to his flock.

PSALM 100:3 NIRV

Here I am! I stand at the door and knock. If anyone hears my voice and opens the door, I will come in and eat with him, and he with me.

REVELATION 3:20

"You are my friends if you obey me. I no longer call you servants, because a master doesn't confide in his servants. Now you are my friends, since I have told you everything the Father told me. You didn't choose me. I chose you. I appointed you to go and produce fruit that will last, so that the Father will give you whatever you ask for, using my name."

JOHN 15:14–16 NLT

"Remember, I am with you always, to the end of the age."

MATTHEW 28:20 NRSV

LONELINESS

Father of the fatherless and protector of widows is God in his holy habitation. God gives the desolate a home to dwell in; he leads out the prisoners to prosperity; but the rebellious dwell in a parched land.

PSALM 68:5–6 RSV

Two are better than one, because they have a good reward for their labor. For if they fall, the one will lift up his fellow; but woe to him who is alone when he falls, and doesn't have another to lift him up. Again, if two lie together, then they have warmth; but how can one keep warm alone? If a man prevails against one who is alone, two shall withstand him; and a threefold cord is not quickly broken.

ECCLESIASTES 4:9–12 WEB

I will not leave you as orphans [comfortless, desolate, bereaved, forlorn, helpless]; I will come [back] to you.

JOHN 14:18 AB

The LORD is kind to everyone who trusts and obeys him.

LAMENTATIONS 3:25 CEV

The LORD protects the strangers; He supports the fatherless and the widow, but He thwarts the way of the wicked.

PSALM 146:9 NASB

199

LONELINESS

Can a mother forget the infant at her breast, walk away from the baby she bore? But even if mothers forget, I'd never forget you—never. Look, I've written your names on the backs of my hands. The walls you're rebuilding are never out of my sight.

ISAIAH 49:15–16 MSG

My God will use his wonderful riches in Christ Jesus to give you everything you need.

PHILIPPIANS 4:19 NCV

The LORD is near to all who call upon Him, to all who call upon Him in truth.

PSALM 145:18 NKJV

Even a man who has many companions can be destroyed. But there is a friend who sticks closer than a brother.

PROVERBS 18:24 NIRV

I will betroth you to me forever; I will betroth you in righteousness and justice, in love and compassion. I will betroth you in faithfulness, and you will acknowledge the LORD.

HOSEA 2:19–20

LONELINESS

For God has said, "I will never fail you. I will never forsake you."

HEBREWS 13:5 NLT

Come close to God and He will come close to you.

JAMES 4:8 AB

Turn to me and be gracious to me, for I am lonely and afflicted.

PSALM 25:16 NRSV

Therefore, "'Come out from among them, and be separate,' says the Lord, 'Touch no unclean thing. I will receive you. I will be to you a Father. You will be to me sons and daughters,' says the Lord Almighty."

2 CORINTHIANS 6:17–18 WEB

Then you shall call, and the LORD will answer; you shall cry, and he will say, "Here I am."

ISAIAH 58:9 RSV

And you are fully grown because you belong to Christ, who is over every power and authority.

COLOSSIANS 2:10 CEV

"And when two or three of you are together because of me, you can be sure that I'll be there."

MATTHEW 18:20 MSG

My soul longed and even yearned for the courts of the LORD; My heart and my flesh sing for joy to the living God.... How blessed are those who dwell in Your house! They are ever praising You. For a day in Your courts is better than a thousand outside. I would rather stand at the threshold of the house of my God than dwell in the tents of wickedness.

PSALM 84:2, 4, 10 NASB

In every man there is a loneliness, an inner chamber
of peculiar life into which God only can enter.
—GEORGE MACDONALD

A STUDENT RELIES ON GOD REGARDING ...

LOSS

I do not want you to be ignorant, brethren, concerning those who have fallen asleep, lest you sorrow as others who have no hope. For if we believe that Jesus died and rose again, even so God will bring with Him those who sleep in Jesus.

1 THESSALONIANS 4:13–14 NKJV

Those who are right with God die. And no one really cares about it. Men who are faithful to the Lord are swept away by trouble. And no one understands why that happens to those who do what is right. Those who lead honest lives will enjoy peace and rest when they die.

ISAIAH 57:1–2 NIRV

The thief comes only to steal and kill and destroy; I have come that they may have life, and have it to the full.

JOHN 10:10

I will call to you whenever trouble strikes, and you will answer me.

PSALM 86:7 NLT

LOSS

I will repay you for the years that the swarming locust has eaten, the hopper, the destroyer, and the cutter, my great army, which I sent against you. You shall eat in plenty and be satisfied, and praise the name of the Lord your God, who has dealt wondrously with you. And my people shall never again be put to shame.

JOEL 2:25–26 NRSV

But I am afflicted and in pain; let thy salvation, O God, set me on high! I will praise the name of God with a song; I will magnify him with thanksgiving.... Let the oppressed see it and be glad; you who seek God, let your hearts revive. For the LORD hears the needy, and does not despise his own that are in bonds.

PSALM 69:29–30, 32–33 RSV

The cords of death surrounded me. The floods of ungodliness made me afraid. In my distress I called on [the Lord], and cried to my God. He heard my voice out of his temple, my cry before him came into his ears.

PSALM 18:4, 6 WEB

LOSS

O death, where is your victory? O death, where is your sting? Now sin is the sting of death, and sin exercises its power [upon the soul] through [the abuse of] the Law. But thanks be to God, Who gives us the victory [making us conquerors] through our Lord Jesus Christ.

I CORINTHIANS 15:55–57 AB

You can be sure that anyone who gives up home or brothers or sisters or mother or father or children or land for me and for the good news will be rewarded. In this world they will be given a hundred times as many houses and brothers and sisters and mothers and children and pieces of land, though they will also be mistreated. And in the world to come, they will have eternal life.

MARK 10:29–30 CEV

In times of trouble the wicked are destroyed, but even at death the innocent have faith.

PROVERBS 14:32 CEV

God has a bottle and a book for his people's tears.
What was sown as a tear will come up as a pearl.
—MATTHEW HENRY

MISTAKES

Who then will condemn us? Will Christ Jesus? No, for he is the one who died for us and was raised to life for us and is sitting at the place of highest honor next to God, pleading for us.

ROMANS 8:34 NLT

O Israel, come back! Return to your GOD! You're down but you're not out. "I will heal their waywardness. I will love them lavishly. My anger is played out.

HOSEA 14:1, 4 MSG

Enemy, don't laugh at me. I have fallen, but I will get up again. I sit in the shadow of trouble now, but the LORD will be a light for me.

MICAH 7:8 NCV

The LORD upholds all who fall, and raises up all who are bowed down.

PSALM 145:14 NKJV

Give thanks to God! He always leads us in the winners' parade because we belong to Christ. Through us, God spreads the knowledge of Christ everywhere like perfume.

2 CORINTHIANS 2:14 NIRV

MISTAKES

Though a righteous man falls seven times, he rises again, but the wicked are brought down by calamity.

PROVERBS 24:16

When you go through deep waters and great trouble, I will be with you. When you go through rivers of difficulty, you will not drown! When you walk through the fire of oppression, you will not be burned up; the flames will not consume you. For I am the LORD, your God, the Holy One of Israel, your Savior. I gave Egypt, Ethiopia, and Seba as a ransom for your freedom.

ISAIAH 43:2–3 NLT

Lord, you are good. You are forgiving. You are full of love for all who call out to you.

PSALM 86:5 NIRV

You are merciful, LORD! You are kind and patient and always loving.

PSALM 145:8 CEV

He who conceals his transgressions will not prosper, but he who confesses and forsakes them will obtain mercy.

PROVERBS 28:13 RSV

MISTAKES

Who is a God like you, who pardons iniquity, and passes over the disobedience of the remnant of his heritage? He doesn't retain his anger forever, because he delights in lovingkindness. He will again have compassion on us. He will tread our iniquities under foot; and you will cast all their sins into the depths of the sea.

MICAH 7:18–19 WEB

Return, O faithless sons, [says the Lord, and] I will heal your faithlessness. [And they answer] Behold, we come to You, for You are the Lord our God.

JEREMIAH 3:22 AB

All of us have sinned and fallen short of God's glory. But God treats us much better than we deserve, and because of Christ Jesus, he freely accepts us and sets us free from our sins.

ROMANS 3:23–24 CEV

Humble yourselves under the mighty hand of God, that He may exalt you at the proper time.

1 PETER 5:6 NASB

MISTAKES

As parents feel for their children, GOD feels for those who fear him. He knows us inside and out, keeps in mind that we're made of mud.

PSALM 103:13–14 MSG

But if we confess our sins, he will forgive our sins, because we can trust God to do what is right. He will cleanse us from all the wrongs we have done.

1 JOHN 1:9 NCV

Bless the LORD, O my soul; and all that is within me, bless His holy name! Who redeems your life from destruction, Who crowns you with lovingkindness and tender mercies.

PSALM 103:1, 4 NKJV

We know that in all things God works for the good of those who love him. He appointed them to be saved in keeping with his purpose.

ROMANS 8:28 NIRV

Though he brings grief, he will show compassion, so great is his unfailing love.

LAMENTATIONS 3:32

MISTAKES

For you made us only a little lower than God, and you crowned us with glory and honor. You put us in charge of everything you made, giving us authority over all things.

PSALM 8:5–6 NLT

For you bless the righteous, O Lord; you cover them with favor as with a shield.

PSALM 5:12 NRSV

O LORD, how many are my foes! Many are rising against me; many are saying of me, there is no help for him in God. But thou, O LORD, art a shield about me, my glory, and the lifter of my head. I cry aloud to the LORD, and he answers me from his holy hill.

PSALM 3:1–4 RSV

Being confident of this very thing, that he who began a good work in you will complete it until the day of Jesus Christ.

PHILIPPIANS 1:6 WEB

MISTAKES

Who shall ever separate us from Christ's love? Shall suffering and affliction and tribulation? Or calamity and distress? Or persecution or hunger or destitution or peril or sword? Yet amid all these things we are more than conquerors and gain a surpassing victory through Him Who loved us.

ROMANS 8:35, 37 AB

The LORD will hold your hand, and if you stumble, you still won't fall.

PSALM 37:24 CEV

The LORD favors those who fear Him, those who wait for His lovingkindness.

PSALM 147:11 NASB

A life spent in making mistakes is not only more honorable but more useful than a life spent doing nothing.
—GEORGE BERNARD SHAW

PRIDE

Humble yourselves [feeling very insignificant] in the presence of the Lord, and He will exalt you [He will lift you up and make your lives significant].

JAMES 4:10 AB

First pride, then the crash—the bigger the ego, the harder the fall. It's better to live humbly among the poor than to live it up among the rich and famous.

PROVERBS 16:18–19 MSG

These are the ways of the world: wanting to please our sinful selves, wanting the sinful things we see, and being too proud of what we have. None of these come from the Father, but all of them come from the world. The world and everything that people want in it are passing away, but the person who does what God wants lives forever.

1 JOHN 2:16–17 NCV

You will save the humble people, but will bring down haughty looks.

PSALM 18:27 NKJV

Foolish people are punished for what they say. But the things wise people say keep them safe.

PROVERBS 14:3 NIRV

PRIDE

When pride comes, then comes disgrace, but with humility comes wisdom.

PROVERBS 11:2

Stop acting so proud and haughty! Don't speak with such arrogance! The LORD is a God who knows your deeds; and he will judge you for what you have done.

1 SAMUEL 2:3 NLT

With the loyal you show yourself loyal; with the blameless you show yourself blameless; with the pure you show yourself pure, and with the crooked you show yourself perverse. You deliver a humble people, but your eyes are upon the haughty to bring them down.

2 SAMUEL 22:26–28 NRSV

He that is down needs fear no fall,
He that is low, no pride;
He that is humble ever shall
Have God to be his guide.
—JOHN BUNYAN

REJECTION

Yes, my own familiar friend, in whom I trusted, who ate bread with me, has lifted up his heel against me.

PSALM 41:9–11 WEB

Blessed are those who are persecuted for righteousness' sake, for theirs is the kingdom of heaven.

MATTHEW 5:10 RSV

You shall also be [so beautiful and prosperous as to be thought of as] a crown of glory and honor in the hand of the Lord, and a royal diadem [exceedingly beautiful] in the hand of your God. You [Judah] shall no more be termed Forsaken, nor shall your land be called Desolate any more. But you shall be called Hephzibah [My delight is in her], and your land be called Beulah [married]; for the Lord delights in you, and your land shall be married [owned and protected by the Lord].

ISAIAH 62:3–4 AB

You are merciful and kind, and so you never forgot them or let them be destroyed. Our God, you are powerful, fearsome, and faithful, always true to your word. So please keep in mind the terrible sufferings of our people, kings, leaders, priests, and prophets, from the time Assyria ruled until this very day.

NEHEMIAH 9:31–32 CEV

214

REJECTION

I call upon the LORD, who is worthy to be praised, and I am saved from my enemies.

PSALM 18:3 NASB

Don't lose your grip on Love and Loyalty. Tie them around your neck; carve their initials on your heart. Earn a reputation for living well in God's eyes and the eyes of the people.

PROVERBS 3:3–4 MSG

There you can look for the LORD your God, and you will find him if you look for him with your whole being. It will be hard when all these things happen to you. But after that you will come back to the LORD your God and obey him, because the LORD your God is a merciful God. He will not leave you or destroy you. He will not forget the Agreement with your ancestors, which he swore to them.

DEUTERONOMY 4:29–31 NCV

"I will restore health to you and heal you of your wounds," says the LORD, "Because they called you an outcast saying 'This is Zion; No one seeks her.'"

JEREMIAH 30:17 NKJV

REJECTION

You didn't receive a spirit that makes you a slave to fear once again. Instead you received the Holy Spirit, who makes you God's child. By the Spirit's power we call God "Abba." Abba means Father. The Spirit himself joins with our spirits. Together they give witness that we are God's children.

ROMANS 8:15–16 NIRV

He was despised and rejected by men; a man of sorrows, and acquainted with grief; and as one from whom men hide their faces he was despised, and we esteemed him not. Surely he has borne our griefs and carried our sorrows; yet we esteemed him stricken, smitten by God, and afflicted. But he was wounded for our transgressions, he was bruised for our iniquities; upon him was the chastisement that made us whole, and with his stripes we are healed.

ISAIAH 53:3–5 RSV

All that the Father gives me will come to me, and whoever comes to me I will never drive away.

JOHN 6:37

REJECTION

Let all who take refuge in you rejoice; let them sing joyful praises forever. Protect them, so all who love your name may be filled with joy. For you bless the godly, O LORD, surrounding them with your shield of love.

PSALM 5:11-12 NLT

When the ways of people please the Lord, he causes even their enemies to be at peace with them.

PROVERBS 16:7 NRSV

For [the Lord] won't reject his people, neither will he forsake his inheritance.

PSALM 94:14 WEB

Fools make a mock of sin and sin mocks the fools [who are its victims; a sin offering made by them only mocks them, bringing them disappointment and disfavor], but among the upright there is the favor of God.

PROVERBS 14:9 AB

The LORD has chosen you to be his own people. He will always take care of you so that everyone will know how great he is.

I SAMUEL 12:22 CEV

217

REJECTION

No one understands you, your friends reproach;
but your Maker draws nigh, and gives you a song—
a song of hope, the song which is harmonious
with the strong, deep music of His providence.
Be ready to sing the songs that your Mother gives.
—LETTIE B. COWMAN

A STUDENT RELIES ON GOD REGARDING ... ◆ ◆
RELATIONSHIPS

"Again I say to you, that if two of you agree on earth about anything that they may ask, it shall be done for them by My Father who is in heaven. For where two or three have gathered together in My name, I am there in their midst."

MATTHEW 18:19–20 NASB

Servants, do what you're told by your earthly masters. And don't just do the minimum that will get you by. Do your best. Work from the heart for your real Master, for God, confident that you'll get paid in full when you come into your inheritance. Keep in mind always that the ultimate Master you're serving is Christ.

COLOSSIANS 3:22–24 MSG

God, who has called you to share everything with his Son, Jesus Christ our Lord, is faithful.

1 CORINTHIANS 1:9 NCV

RELATIONSHIPS

Two are better than one, because they have a good reward for their labor. For if they fall, one will lift up his companion. But woe to him who is alone when he falls, for he has no one to help him up. Again, if two lie down together, they will keep warm; but how can one be warm alone? Though one may be overpowered by another, two can withstand him. And a threefold cord is not quickly broken.

ECCLESIASTES 4:9–12 NKJV

Scripture says, "Honor your father and mother." That is the first commandment that has a promise. "Then things will go well with you. You will live a long time on the earth."

EPHESIANS 6:2–3 NIRV

By wisdom a house is built, and through understanding it is established; through knowledge its rooms are filled with rare and beautiful treasures.

PROVERBS 24:3–4

If we are living in the light of God's presence, just as Christ is, then we have fellowship with each other, and the blood of Jesus, his Son, cleanses us from every sin.

1 JOHN 1:7 NLT

RELATIONSHIPS

Don't become partners with those who reject God. How can you make a partnership out of right and wrong? That's not partnership; that's war. Is light best friends with dark? Does Christ go strolling with the Devil? Do trust and mistrust hold hands? Who would think of setting up pagan idols in God's holy Temple? But that is exactly what we are, each of us a temple in whom God lives. God himself put it this way: "I'll live in them, move into them; I'll be their God and they'll be my people. So leave the corruption and compromise; leave it for good," says God. "Don't link up with those who will pollute you. I want you all for myself. I'll be a Father to you; you'll be sons and daughters to me."

2 CORINTHIANS 6:14–18 MSG

The good leave an inheritance to their children's children, but the sinner's wealth is laid up for the righteous.

PROVERBS 13:22 NRSV

Grandchildren are the crown of the aged, and the glory of sons is their fathers.

PROVERBS 17:6 RSV

RELATIONSHIPS

Don't forsake your friend and your father's friend. Don't go to your brother's house in the day of your disaster: Better is a neighbor who is near than a distant brother.

PROVERBS 27:10 WEB

For thus says the Lord: To the eunuchs who keep My Sabbaths and choose the things which please Me and hold firmly My covenant—to them I will give in My house and within My walls a memorial and a name better [and more enduring] than sons and daughters; I will give them an everlasting name that will not be cut off.

ISAIAH 56:4–5 AB

Foreigners will follow me. They will love me and worship in my name; they will respect the Sabbath and keep our agreement. I will bring them to my holy mountain, where they will celebrate in my house of worship. Their sacrifices and offerings will always be welcome on my altar. Then my house will be known as a house of worship for all nations.

ISAIAH 56:6–7 CEV

RELATIONSHIPS

"Then the King will say to those on his right, 'Enter, you who are blessed by my Father! Take what's coming to you in this kingdom. It's been ready for you since the world's foundation. And here's why: I was hungry and you fed me, I was thirsty and you gave me a drink, I was homeless and you gave me a room, I was shivering and you gave me clothes, I was sick and you stopped to visit, I was in prison and you came to me.'"

MATTHEW 25:34–36 MSG

Jesus answered, "'Love the Lord your God with all your heart, all your soul, and all your mind.' This is the first and most important command. And the second command is like the first: 'Love your neighbor as you love yourself.' All the law and the writings of the prophets depend on these two commands."

MATTHEW 22:37–40 NCV

Let us be first to give a friendship sign, to nod first,
smile first, speak first, and if such a thing
is necessary—forgive first.
—UNKNOWN

223

SELF-ESTEEM

Show Your marvelous lovingkindness by Your right hand, O You who save those who trust in You from those who rise up against them. Keep me as the apple of Your eye; hide me under the shadow of Your wings.

PSALM 17:7–8 NKJV

The Lord created you.... He formed you. He says, "Do not be afraid. I will set you free. I will send for you by name. You belong to me."

ISAIAH 43:1 NIRV

How precious to me are your thoughts, O God! How vast is the sum of them! Were I to count them, they would outnumber the grains of sand. When I awake, I am still with you.

PSALM 139:17–18

"I have written your name on my hand."

ISAIAH 49:16 NLT

SELF-ESTEEM

What is a human being that you think about him? What is a son of man that you take care of him? You made him a little lower than the heavenly beings. You placed on him a crown of glory and honor. You made human beings the rulers over all that your hands have created. You put everything under their control.

PSALM 8:4–6 NIRV

"I have loved you with an everlasting love; therefore I have continued my faithfulness to you."

JEREMIAH 31:3 RSV

You formed my inmost being. You knit me together in my mother's womb.

PSALM 139:13 WEB

Consider then thyself, O noble soul, and the nobility within thee, for thou art honored above all creatures in that thou art an image of God; … thou art destined to greatness!
—MEISTER ECKHART

225

A STUDENT RELIES ON GOD REGARDING ...
SELFISHNESS

"Give, and [gifts] will be given to you; good measure, pressed down, shaken together, and running over, will they pour into [the pouch formed by] the bosom [of your robe and used as a bag]. For with the measure you deal out [with the measure you use when you confer benefits on others], it will be measured back to you."

LUKE 6:38 AB

"If you want to be great, you must be the servant of all the others. And if you want to be first, you must be everyone's slave. The Son of Man did not come to be a slave master, but a slave who will give his life to rescue many people."

MARK 10:43–45 CEV

"In everything, therefore, treat people the same way you want them to treat you, for this is the Law and the Prophets."

MATTHEW 7:12 NASB

"The servant who knows what his master wants and ignores it, or insolently does whatever he pleases, will be thoroughly thrashed. But if he does a poor job through ignorance, he'll get off with a slap on the hand. Great gifts mean great responsibilities; greater gifts, greater responsibilities!"

LUKE 12:48 MSG

SELFISHNESS

Being kind to the poor is like lending to the LORD; he will reward you for what you have done.

PROVERBS 19:17 NCV

The righteous considers the cause of the poor, but the wicked does not understand such knowledge.

PROVERBS 29:7 NKJV

"What I'm about to tell you is true. Anything you did for one of the least important of these brothers of mine, you did for me."

MATTHEW 25:40 NIRV

He who gives to the poor will lack nothing, but he who closes his eyes to them receives many curses.

PROVERBS 28:27

Those who shut their ears to the cries of the poor will be ignored in their own time of need.

PROVERBS 21:13 NLT

Those who are generous are blessed, for they share their bread with the poor.

PROVERBS 22:9 NRSV

SELFISHNESS

Do nothing from selfishness or conceit, but in humility count others better than yourselves. Let each of you look not only to his own interests, but also to the interests of others. Have this mind among yourselves, which is yours in Christ Jesus, who, though he was in the form of God, did not count equality with God a thing to be grasped, but emptied himself, taking the form of a servant, being born in the likeness of men.

PHILIPPIANS 2:3–7 RSV

It is more blessed to give than to receive.

ACTS 20:35 WEB

It [love] is not conceited (arrogant and inflated with pride); it is not rude (unmannerly) and does not act unbecomingly. Love (God's love in us) does not insist on its own rights or its own way, for it is not self-seeking; it is not touchy or fretful or resentful; it takes no account of the evil done to it [it pays no attention to a suffered wrong].

I CORINTHIANS 13:5 AB

SELFISHNESS

What we have done for ourselves alone dies with us;
what we have done for others and the world remains
and is eternal.
—ALBERT PIKE

SHAME

Keep your eyes on the LORD! You will shine like the sun and never blush with shame. I was a nobody, but I prayed, and the LORD saved me from all my troubles.

PSALM 34:5–6 CEV

If we walk in the Light as He Himself is in the Light, we have fellowship with one another, and the blood of Jesus His Son cleanses us from all sin.

1 JOHN 1:7 NASB

All who are hunting for you—oh, let them sing and be happy. Let those who know what you're all about tell the world you're great and not quitting.

PSALM 40:16 MSG

You are pure to those who are pure, but you are against those who are bad. You save the humble, but you bring down those who are proud. Lord, you give light to my lamp. My God brightens the darkness around me.

PSALM 18:26–28 NCV

Fine linen, bright and clean, was given to her to wear. Fine linen stands for the right things that God's people do.

REVELATION 19:8 NIRV

SHAME

What agreement has the temple of God with idols? For you are the temple of the living God. As God has said: "I will dwell in them and walk among them. I will be their God, and they shall be My people." ... Therefore, having these promises, beloved, let us cleanse ourselves from all filthiness of the flesh and spirit, perfecting holiness in the fear of God.

2 CORINTHIANS 6:16, 7:1 NKJV

Husbands, love your wives, just as Christ loved the church and gave himself up for her. to make her holy, cleansing her by the washing with water through the word, and to present her to himself as a radiant church, without stain or wrinkle or any other blemish, but holy and blameless.

EPHESIANS 5:25–27

Give the people of Israel this message from the Sovereign LORD: I am bringing you back again but not because you deserve it. I am doing it to protect my holy name, which you dishonored while you were scattered among the nations.... Then I will sprinkle clean water on you, and you will be clean. Your filth will be washed away, and you will no longer worship idols. And I will give you a new heart with new and right desires, and I will put a new spirit in you. I will take out your stony heart of sin and give you a new, obedient heart. And I will put my Spirit in

SHAME

you so you will obey my laws and do whatever I command....
I will cleanse you of your filthy behavior. I will give you good
crops, and I will abolish famine in the land.

EZEKIEL 36:22, 25–27, 29 NLT

"I will cleanse them from all the guilt of their sin against me,
and I will forgive all the guilt of their sin and rebellion
against me."

JEREMIAH 33:8 NRSV

The LORD, your God, is in your midst, a warrior who gives
victory; he will rejoice over you with gladness, he will renew
you in his love; he will exult over you with loud singing as on
a day of festival. "I will remove disaster from you, so that you
will not bear reproach for it. Behold, at that time I will deal
with all your oppressors. And I will save the lame and gather
the outcast, and I will change their shame into praise and
renown in all the earth."

ZEPHANIAH 3:17–19 RSV

[Lord,] draw near to my soul, and redeem it. Ransom me
because of my enemies. You know my reproach, my shame,
and my dishonor. My adversaries are all before you.

PSALM 69:18–19 WEB

SHAME

A gracious and good woman wins honor [for her husband], and violent men win riches but a woman who hates righteousness is a throne of dishonor for him.

PROVERBS 11:16 AB

Dedicate yourselves to me and be holy because I am the LORD your God. I have chosen you as my people, and I expect you to obey my laws.

LEVITICUS 20:7–8 CEV

For the Scripture says, "WHOEVER BELIEVES IN HIM WILL NOT BE DISAPPOINTED."

ROMANS 10:11 NASB

Then I will not be disgraced when I compare my life with your commands.... How can a young person stay pure? By obeying your word and following its rules.

PSALM 119:6, 9 NLT

As it is written in the Scripture: "I will put in Jerusalem a stone that causes people to stumble, a rock that makes them fall. Anyone who trusts in him will never be disappointed."

ROMANS 9:33 NCV

SHAME

True humility accepts the love that is bestowed upon it, and the gifts of that love, with a meek and happy thankfulness, while pride shrinks from accepting gifts and kindnesses, and is afraid to believe in the disinterested goodness of the one who bestows them. Were we truly humble, we would accept God's love with thankful meekness, and, while acknowledging our own unworthiness, would only think of it as enhancing His grace and goodness in choosing us as the recipients of such blessings.

—HANNAH WHITALL SMITH

A STUDENT RELIES ON GOD REGARDING ... ◆ ◆
STRESS

We do not want you to be uninformed, brethren, about the affliction and oppressing distress which befell us in [the province of] Asia, how we were so utterly and unbearably weighed down and crushed that we despaired even of life [itself]. Indeed, we felt within ourselves that we had received the [very] sentence of death, but that was to keep us from trusting in and depending on ourselves instead of on God Who raises the dead.[For it is He] Who rescued and saved us from such a perilous death, and He will still rescue and save us; in and on Him we have set our hope (our joyful and confident expectation) that He will again deliver us [from danger and destruction and draw us to Himself].

2 CORINTHIANS 1:8–10 AB

"Come to Me, all you who labor and are heavy laden, and I will give you rest. Take My yoke upon you and learn from Me, for I am gentle and lowly in heart, and you will find rest for your souls. For My yoke is easy and My burden is light."

MATTHEW 11:28–30 NKJV

He gives strength to the weary and increases the power of the weak.

ISAIAH 40:29

STRESS

Then you called out to GOD in your desperate condition; he got you out in the nick of time. He quieted the wind down to a whisper, put a muzzle on all the big waves. And you were so glad when the storm died down, and he led you safely back to harbor.

PSALM 107:28–30 MSG

Even children become tired and need to rest, and young people trip and fall. But the people who trust the LORD will become strong again. They will rise up as an eagle in the sky; they will run and not need rest; they will walk and not become tired.

ISAIAH 40:30–31 NCV

I said, "My foot is slipping." But Lord, your love kept me from falling. I was very worried. But your comfort brought joy to my heart.

PSALM 94:18–19 NIRV

Be still, and know that I am God; I will be exalted among the nations, I will be exalted in the earth! The LORD of hosts is with us; The God of Jacob is our refuge.

PSALM 46:10–11 NKJV

[Jesus] got up, rebuked the wind and said to the waves, "Quiet! Be still!" Then the wind died down and it was completely calm. He said to his disciples, "Why are you so afraid? Do you still have no faith?" They were terrified and asked each other, "Who is this? Even the wind and the waves obey him!"

MARK 4:39–41

Drop thy still dews of quietness,
Till all our strivings cease;
Take from our souls the strain and stress,
And let our ordered lives confess
The beauty of thy peace.
—JOHN GREENLEAF WHITTIER

TEMPTATION

And now, all glory to God, who is able to keep you from stumbling, and who will bring you into his glorious presence innocent of sin and with great joy.

JUDE V. 24 NLT

He gives all the more grace; therefore it says, "God opposes the proud, but gives grace to the humble." Submit yourselves therefore to God. Resist the devil, and he will flee from you.

JAMES 4:6–7 NRSV

Then the Lord knows how to rescue the godly from trial, and to keep the unrighteous under punishment until the day of judgment.

2 PETER 2:9 RSV

Little children, you are of God [you belong to Him] and have [already] defeated and overcome them [the agents of the antichrist], because He Who lives in you is greater (mightier) than he who is in the world.

I JOHN 4:4 AB

TEMPTATION

Neither grumble, as some of them also grumbled, and perished by the destroyer. Now all these things happened to them by way of example, and they were written for our admonition, on whom the ends of the ages have come. Therefore let him who thinks he stands be careful that he doesn't fall. No temptation has taken you but such as man can bear. God is faithful, who will not allow you to be tempted above what you are able, but will with the temptation make also the way of escape, that you may be able to endure it.

I CORINTHIANS 10:10–13 WEB

Don't let sin keep ruling your lives. You are ruled by God's kindness and not by the Law.

ROMANS 6:14 CEV

Consider it a sheer gift, friends, when tests and challenges come at you from all sides. You know that under pressure, your faith-life is forced into the open and shows its true colors. So don't try to get out of anything prematurely. Let it do its work so you become mature and well-developed, not deficient in any way.... Anyone who meets a testing challenge head-on and manages to stick it out is mighty fortunate. For such persons loyally in love with God, the reward is life and more life.

JAMES 1:2–4, 12 MSG

TEMPTATION

Don't depend on your own wisdom. Respect the LORD and refuse to do wrong. Then your body will be healthy, and your bones will be strong.

PROVERBS 3:7–8 NCV

Hate evil, you who love the LORD, Who preserves the souls of His godly ones; He delivers them from the hand of the wicked.

PSALM 97:10 NASB

We do not have a High Priest who cannot sympathize with our weaknesses, but was in all points tempted as we are, yet without sin. Let us therefore come boldly to the throne of grace, that we may obtain mercy and find grace to help in time of need.

HEBREWS 4:15–16 NKJV

God is a safe place to hide, ready to help when we need him.

PSALM 46:1 MSG

He himself suffered when he was tempted. Now he is able to help others who are being tempted.

HEBREWS 2:18 NIRV

TEMPTATION

Carefully guard your thoughts because they are the source of true life.

PROVERBS 4:23 CEV

I seek you with all my heart; do not let me stray from your commands. I have hidden your word in my heart that I might not sin against you.

PSALM 119:10–11

Have mercy on me, O God, because of your unfailing love. Because of your great compassion, blot out the stain of my sins. Wash me clean from my guilt. Purify me from my sin. For I recognize my shameful deeds—they haunt me day and night.... But you desire honesty from the heart, so you can teach me to be wise in my inmost being.

PSALM 51:1–3, 6 NLT

No one, when tempted, should say, "I am being tempted by God"; for God cannot be tempted by evil and he himself tempts no one. But one is tempted by one's own desire, being lured and enticed by it.

JAMES 1:13–14 NRSV

TEMPTATION

My eyes are ever on [the Lord], for he will pluck my feet out of the net. Turn to me, and have mercy on me, for I am desolate and afflicted. The troubles of my heart are enlarged. Oh bring me out of my distresses. Consider my affliction and my travail. Forgive all my sins. Consider my enemies, for they are many. They hate me with cruel hatred. Oh keep my soul, and deliver me. Let me not be put to shame, for I take refuge in you. Let integrity and uprightness preserve me, for I wait for you.

PSALM 25:15–21 WEB

Who can discern his errors? Clear thou me from hidden faults. Keep back thy servant also from presumptuous sins; let them not have dominion over me! Then I shall be blameless, and innocent of great transgression.

PSALM 19:12–13 RSV

TEMPTATION

For skillful and godly Wisdom shall enter into your heart, and knowledge shall be pleasant to you. Discretion shall watch over you, understanding shall keep you, to deliver you from the way of evil and the evil men, from men who speak perverse things and are liars, men who forsake the paths of uprightness to walk in the ways of darkness, ... [Discretion shall watch over you, understanding shall keep you] to deliver you from the alien woman, from the outsider with her flattering words, who forsakes the husband and guide of her youth and forgets the covenant of her God.

PROVERBS 2:10–13, 16–17 AB

To attempt to resist temptation, abandon bad habits, and control passion in our own strength, is like attempting to check by a spider's thread the progress of a ship.
—BENJAMIN WAUGH

WORRY

Don't worry and ask yourselves, "Will we have anything to eat? Will we have anything to drink? Will we have any clothes to wear?" Only people who don't know God are always worrying about such things. Your Father in heaven knows that you need all of these. But more than anything else, put God's work first and do what he wants. Then the other things will be yours as well.

MATTHEW 6:31–33 CEV

Without leadership a nation falls, but lots of good advice will save it.

PROVERBS 11:14 NCV

I will listen to you, LORD God, because you promise peace to those who are faithful and no longer foolish.

PSALM 85:8 CEV

I will both lie down in peace, and sleep; For You alone, O LORD, make me dwell in safety.

PSALM 4:8 NKJV

Therefore, brethren, be all the more diligent to make certain about His calling and choosing you; for as long as you practice these things, you will never stumble.

2 PETER 1:10 NASB

WORRY

Lord, you are like a shield that keeps me safe. You help me win the battle. Your strong right hand keeps me going. You bend down to make me great. You give me a wide path to walk on so that I don't twist my ankles.

PSALM 18:35–36 NIRV

Surely God is my salvation; I will trust and not be afraid. The LORD, the LORD, is my strength and my song; he has become my salvation.

ISAIAH 12:2

For God has not given us a spirit of fear and timidity, but of power, love, and self-discipline.

2 TIMOTHY 1:7 NLT

My child, do not let these escape from your sight: keep sound wisdom and prudence.... If you sit down, you will not be afraid; when you lie down, your sleep will be sweet.

PROVERBS 3:21, 24 NRSV

Humble yourselves therefore under the mighty hand of God, that in due time he may exalt you. Cast all your anxieties on him, for he cares about you.

1 PETER 5:6–7 RSV

WORRY

Don't fret or worry. Instead of worrying, pray. Let petitions and praises shape your worries into prayers, letting God know your concerns. Before you know it, a sense of God's wholeness, everything coming together for good, will come and settle you down. It's wonderful what happens when Christ displaces worry at the center of your life.

PHILIPPIANS 4:6-7 MSG

Blessed is the man who trusts in [the Lord], and whose trust [the Lord] is. For he shall be as a tree planted by the waters, who spreads out its roots by the river, and shall not fear when heat comes, but its leaf shall be green; and shall not be careful in the year of drought, neither shall cease from yielding fruit.

JEREMIAH 17:7-8 WEB

Your word is a lamp to my feet and a light to my path.

PSALM 119:105 AB

Quick is the succession of human events; the cares of today are seldom the cares of tomorrow; and when we lie down at night, we may safely say to most of our troubles, "You have done your worst, and we shall meet no more."

—WILLIAM COWPER

31 SCRIPTURE AFFIRMATIONS FOR A TRANSFORMED YOU

A BIT OF THE BOOK IN THE MORNING,
TO ORDER MY ONWARD WAY.
A BIT OF THE BOOK IN THE EVENING,
TO HALLOW THE END OF THE DAY.

—MARGARET SANGSTER

DO NOT BE CONFORMED TO THIS WORLD, BUT BE
TRANSFORMED BY THE RENEWING OF YOUR MIND, SO THAT YOU
MAY PROVE WHAT THE WILL OF GOD IS, THAT WHICH IS GOOD
AND ACCEPTABLE AND PERFECT.

—ROMANS 12:2 NASB

FOR A TRANSFORMED YOU

DAY 1

God did not send his Son into the world to condemn its people. He sent him to save them!

JOHN 3:17 CEV

DAY 2

It is God who is at work in you, both to will and to work for His good pleasure.

PHILIPPIANS 2:13 NASB

DAY 3

That's why we can be so sure that every detail in our lives of love for God is worked into something good.

ROMANS 8:28 MSG

DAY 4

God did not give us a spirit that makes us afraid but a spirit of power and love and self-control.

2 TIMOTHY 1:7 NCV

DAY 5

If any of you lack wisdom, let him ask of God, that giveth to all men liberally, and upbraideth not; and it shall be given him.

JAMES 1:5 KJV

DAY 6

I sought the LORD, and he answered me; he delivered me from all my fears.

PSALM 34:4

DAY 7

So do not fear, for I am with you; do not be dismayed, for I am your God. I will strengthen you and help you; I will uphold you with my righteous right hand.

ISAIAH 41:10

DAY 8

If we confess our sins to him, he is faithful and just to forgive us and to cleanse us from every wrong.

1 JOHN 1:9 NLT

DAY 9

Bless the Lord, O my soul, and do not forget all his benefits—who forgives all your iniquity, who heals all your diseases.

PSALM 103:2–3 NRSV

DAY 10

This is the boldness which we have toward him, that, if we ask anything according to his will, he listens to us. And if we know that he listens to us whatever we ask, we know that we have the petitions which we have asked of him.

1 JOHN 5:14–15 WEB

DAY 11

His divine power has granted to us all things that pertain to life and godliness, through the knowledge of him who called us to his own glory and excellence.

2 PETER 1:3 RSV

DAY 12

Peace I leave with you; My [own] peace I now give and bequeath to you. Not as the world gives do I give to you. Do not let your hearts be troubled, neither let them be afraid. [Stop allowing yourselves to be agitated and disturbed; and do not permit yourselves to be fearful and intimidated and cowardly and unsettled.]

JOHN 14:27 AB

DAY 13

God is the one who began this good work in you, and I am certain that he won't stop before it is complete on the day that Christ Jesus returns.

PHILIPPIANS 1:6 CEV

FOR A TRANSFORMED YOU

DAY 14

The LORD is my light and my salvation; whom shall I fear?
The LORD is the defense of my life; whom shall I dread?

PSALM 27:1 NASB

DAY 15

People with their minds set on you, you keep completely whole,
steady on their feet, because they keep at it and don't quit.

ISAIAH 26:3 MSG

DAY 16

You will teach me how to live a holy life. Being with you
will fill me with joy; at your right hand I will find pleasure
forever.

PSALM 16:11 NCV

DAY 17

And my God shall supply all your need according to His
riches in glory by Christ Jesus.

PHILIPPIANS 4:19 NKJV

DAY 18

Give all your worries and cares to God, for he cares about what happens to you.

1 PETER 5:7 NLT

DAY 19

This is what the LORD says—your Redeemer, the Holy One of Israel: "I am the LORD your God, who teaches you what is best for you, who directs you in the way you should go."

ISAIAH 48:17

DAY 20

Christ set us free from the curse of the law. He did it by becoming a curse for us. It is written, "Everyone who is hung on a pole is under God's curse." Christ Jesus set us free so that the blessing given to Abraham would come to non-Jews through Christ. He did it so that we might receive the promise of the Holy Spirit by believing in Christ.

GALATIANS 3:13–14 NIRV

DAY 21

If you abide in me, and my words abide in you, ask for whatever you wish, and it will be done for you.

JOHN 15:7 NRSV

DAY 22

Thou hast turned for me my mourning into dancing; thou hast loosed my sackcloth and girded me with gladness.

PSALM 30:11 RSV

DAY 23

Give, and it will be given to you, good measure, pressed down, shaken together, and running over, will they give into your bosom. For with the same measure you measure it will be measured back to you.

LUKE 6:38 WEB

DAY 24

For we are God's [own] handiwork (His workmanship), recreated in Christ Jesus, [born anew] that we may do those good works which God predestined (planned beforehand) for us [taking paths which He prepared ahead of time], that we should walk in them [living the good life which He pre-arranged and made ready for us to live].

EPHESIANS 2:10 AB

DAY 25

His power at work in us can do far more than we dare ask or imagine.

EPHESIANS 3:20 CEV

DAY 26

What then shall we say to these things? If God is for us, who is against us?

ROMANS 8:31 NASB

DAY 27

With the arrival of Jesus, the Messiah, that fateful dilemma is resolved. Those who enter into Christ's being-here-for-us no longer have to live under a continuous, low-lying black cloud.

ROMANS 8:1 MSG

255

DAY 28

I mean that you have been saved by grace through believing.
You did not save yourselves; it was a gift from God.

EPHESIANS 2:8 NCV

DAY 29

I acknowledged my sin to You, and my iniquity I have not
hidden. I said, "I will confess my transgressions to the
LORD," and You forgave the iniquity of my sin.

PSALM 32:5 NKJV

DAY 30

"So I tell you, when you pray for something, believe that you
have already received it. Then it will be yours."

MARK 11:24 NIRV

DAY 31

The one who calls you is faithful and he will do it.

1 THESSALONIANS 5:24

CLASSIC BIBLE PASSAGES FOR MEDITATION

IT IS BY MEDITATION THAT WE RANSACK OUR DEEP AND FALSE HEARTS, FIND OUT OUR SECRET ENEMIES, COME TO GRIPS WITH THEM, EXPEL THEM, AND ARM OURSELVES AGAINST THEIR RE-ENTRANCE. BY MEDITATION, WE MAKE USE OF ALL GOOD MEANS, FIT OURSELVES FOR ALL GOOD DUTIES. BY MEDITATION, WE SEE OUR WEAKNESSES, OBTAIN REDRESS, PREVENT TEMPTATIONS, CHEER UP OUR LONELINESS, TEMPER OUR OCCASIONS OF DELIGHT, GET MORE LIGHT UNTO OUR KNOWLEDGE, ADD MORE HEAT TO OUR AFFECTIONS, PUT MORE LIFE INTO OUR DEVOTIONS. IT IS ONLY BY MEDITATION THAT WE ARE ABLE TO BE STRANGERS UPON THE EARTH AS WE ARE COMMANDED TO BE, AND BY THIS WE ARE BROUGHT TO A RIGHT ESTIMATION OF ALL EARTHLY THINGS. LEARN IT IF YOU CAN, NEGLECT IT IF YOU SO DESIRE, BUT THE ONE WHO DOES SO SHALL NEVER FIND JOY, NEITHER IN GOD, NOR IN THEMSELVES.

-BISHOP JOSEPH HALL

DO NOT LET THIS BOOK OF THE LAW DEPART FROM YOUR MOUTH; MEDITATE ON IT DAY AND NIGHT, SO THAT YOU MAY BE CAREFUL TO DO EVERYTHING WRITTEN IN IT. THEN YOU WILL BE PROSPEROUS AND SUCCESSFUL.

-JOSHUA 1:8

THE TEN COMMANDMENTS

Then God spoke all these words:

"I am the LORD your God, who brought you out of the land of Egypt where you were slaves.

"You must not have any other gods except me.

"You must not make for yourselves an idol that looks like anything in the sky above or on the earth below or in the water below the land. You must not worship or serve any idol, because I, the LORD your God, am a jealous God. If you hate me, I will punish your children, and even your grandchildren and great-grandchildren. But I show kindness to thousands who love me and obey my commands.

"You must not use the name of the LORD your God thoughtlessly; the LORD will punish anyone who misuses his name.

"Remember to keep the Sabbath holy. Work and get everything done during six days each week, but the seventh day is a day of rest to honor the LORD your God. On that day no one may do any work: not you, your son or daughter, your male or female slaves, your animals, or the foreigners living in your cities. The reason is that in six days the LORD made everything—the sky, the earth, the sea, and everything in them. On the seventh day he rested. So the LORD blessed the Sabbath day and made it holy.

"Honor your father and your mother so that you will live a long time in the land that the Lord your God is going to give you.

"You must not murder anyone.

"You must not be guilty of adultery.

"You must not steal.

"You must not tell lies about your neighbor.

"You must not want to take your neighbor's house. You must not want his wife or his male or female slaves, or his ox or his donkey, or anything that belongs to your neighbor."

EXODUS 20:1–17 NCV

A LIFE OF BLESSING

Blessed is the man who does not walk in the counsel of the wicked or stand in the way of sinners or sit in the seat of mockers. But his delight is in the law of the LORD, and on his law he meditates day and night. He is like a tree planted by streams of water, which yields its fruit in season and whose leaf does not wither. Whatever he does prospers. Not so the wicked! They are like chaff that the wind blows away. Therefore the wicked will not stand in the judgment, nor sinners in the assembly of the righteous. For the LORD watches over the way of the righteous, but the way of the wicked will perish.

PSALM 1

PRAYER OF REPENTANCE

God, be merciful to me because you are loving. Because you are always ready to be merciful, wipe out all my wrongs. Wash away all my guilt and make me clean again. I know about my wrongs, and I can't forget my sin. You are the only one I have sinned against; I have done what you say is wrong. You are right when you speak and fair when you judge. I was brought into this world in sin. In sin my mother gave birth to me. You want me to be completely truthful, so teach me wisdom. Take away my sin, and I will be clean. Wash me, and I will be whiter than snow. Make me hear sounds of joy and gladness; let the bones you crushed be happy again. Turn your face from my sins and wipe out all my guilt.

MEDITATION

Create in me a pure heart, God, and make my spirit right again. Do not send me away from you or take your Holy Spirit away from me. Give me back the joy of your salvation. Keep me strong by giving me a willing spirit. Then I will teach your ways to those who do wrong, and sinners will turn back to you. God, save me from the guilt of murder, God of my salvation, and I will sing about your goodness. Lord, let me speak so I may praise you. You are not pleased by sacrifices, or I would give them. You don't want burnt offerings. The sacrifice god wants is a broken spirit. God, you will not reject a heart that is broken and sorry for sin.

PSALM 51:1–17 NCV

THE LORD IS YOUR PROTECTION ❖

He who dwells in the shelter of the Most High will abide in the shadow of the Almighty. I will say to the LORD, "My refuge and my fortress, My God, in whom I trust!" For it is He who delivers you from the snare of the trapper and from the deadly pestilence. He will cover you with His pinions, and under His wings you may seek refuge; His faithfulness is a shield and bulwark. You will not be afraid of the terror by night, or of the arrow that flies by day; of the pestilence that stalks in darkness, or of the destruction that lays waste at noon. A thousand may fall at your side and ten thousand at your right hand, but it shall not approach you. You will only look on with your eyes and see the recompense of the wicked.

For you have made the LORD, my refuge, even the Most High, your dwelling place. No evil will befall you, nor will any plague come near your tent. For He will give His angels charge concerning you, to guard you in all your ways. They will bear you up in their hands, that you do not strike your foot against a stone. You will tread upon the lion and cobra, the young lion and the serpent you will trample down. "Because he has loved Me, therefore I will deliver him; I will set him securely on high, because he has known My name. He will call upon Me, and I will answer him; I will be with him in trouble; I will rescue him and honor him. With a long life I will satisfy him and let him see My salvation."

PSALM 91 NASB

THE LORD SEARCHES AND KNOWS ME

O Lord, you have examined my heart and know everything about me. You know when I sit or stand. When far away you know my every thought. You chart the path ahead of me, and tell me where to stop and rest. Every moment, you know where I am. You know what I am going to say before I even say it. You both precede and follow me, and place your hand of blessing on my head.

This is too glorious, too wonderful to believe! I can never be lost to your Spirit! I can never get away from my God! If I go up to heaven, you are there; if I go down to the place of the dead, you are there. If I ride the morning winds to the farthest oceans, even there your hand will guide me, your strength will support me. If I try to hide in the darkness, the night becomes light around me. For even darkness cannot hide from God; to you the night shines as bright as day. Darkness and light are both alike to you.

You made all the delicate, inner parts of my body and knit them together in my mother's womb. Thank you for making me so wonderfully complex! It is amazing to think about. Your workmanship is marvelous—and how well I know it. You were there while I was being formed in utter seclusion! You saw me before I was born and scheduled each day of my life before I began to breathe. Every day was recorded in your Book!

How precious it is, Lord, to realize that you are thinking about me constantly! I can't even count how many times a day your thoughts turn towards me. And when I waken in the morning, you are still thinking of me!...

Search me, O God, and know my heart; test my thoughts. Point out anything you find in me that makes you sad, and lead me along the path of everlasting life.

PSALM 139:1–18, 23–24 TLB

GOD'S WAYS
ARE HIGHER

❖❖

Ho, everyone who thirsts, come to the waters; and you that have no money, come, buy and eat! Come, buy wine and milk without money and without price. Why do you spend your money for that which is not bread, and your labor for that which does not satisfy? Listen carefully to me, and eat what is good, and delight yourselves in rich food. Incline your ear, and come to me; listen, so that you may live. I will make with you an everlasting covenant, my steadfast, sure love for David....

Seek the Lord while he may be found, call upon him while he is near; let the wicked forsake their way, and the unrighteous their thoughts; let them return to the Lord, that he may have mercy on them, and to our God, for he will abundantly pardon.

MEETATION

For my thoughts are not your thoughts, nor are your ways my ways, says the Lord. For as the heavens are higher than the earth, so are my ways higher than your ways and my thoughts than your thoughts. For as the rain and the snow come down from heaven, and do not return there until they have watered the earth, making it bring forth and sprout, giving seed to the sower and bread to the eater, so shall my word be that goes out from my mouth; it shall not return to me empty, but it shall accomplish that which I purpose, and succeed in the thing for which I sent it. For you shall go out in joy, and be led back in peace; the mountains and the hills before you shall burst into song, and all the trees of the field shall clap their hands.

ISAIAH 55:1–3, 6–12 NRSV

THE BEATITUDES ❖

When Jesus saw the crowds, He went up on the mountain; and after He sat down, His disciples came to Him. He opened His mouth and began to teach them, saying, "Blessed are the poor in spirit, for theirs is the kingdom of heaven. Blessed are those who mourn, for they shall be comforted. Blessed are the gentle, for they shall inherit the earth. Blessed are those who hunger and thirst for righteousness, for they shall be satisfied. Blessed are the merciful, for they shall receive mercy. Blessed are the pure in heart, for they shall see God. Blessed are the peacemakers, for they shall be called sons of God. Blessed are those who have been persecuted for the sake of righteousness, for theirs is the kingdom of heaven. Blessed are you when people insult you and persecute you, and falsely say all kinds of evil against you because of Me. Rejoice and be glad, for your reward in heaven is great; for in the same way they persecuted the prophets who were before you."

MATTHEW 5:1–12 NASB

LOVE YOUR ENEMIES

"You have heard that it was said, 'Love your neighbor and hate your enemy.' But I tell you: Love your enemies and pray for those who persecute you, that you may be sons of your Father in heaven. He causes his sun to rise on the evil and the good, and sends rain on the righteous and the unrighteous. If you love those who love you, what reward will you get? Are not even the tax collectors doing that? And if you greet only your brothers, what are you doing more than others? Do not even pagans do that? Be perfect, therefore, as your heavenly Father is perfect."

MATTHEW 5:43–48

THE LORD'S PRAYER

"In this manner, therefore, pray:

> Our Father in heaven
> Hallowed be Your name.
> Your kingdom come.
> Your will be done
> On earth as it is in heaven.
> Give us this day our daily bread.
> And forgive us our debts,
> As we forgive our debtors.
> And do not lead us into temptation,
> But deliver us from the evil one.
> For Yours is the kingdom and the power
>   and the glory forever. Amen.

"For if you forgive men their trespasses, your heavenly Father will also forgive you. But if you do not forgive men their trespasses, neither will your Father forgive your trespasses."

MATTHEW 6:9–15 NKJV

LOVE IS . . .

If I speak with human eloquence and angelic ecstasy but don't love, I'm nothing but the creaking of a rusty gate. If I speak God's Word with power, revealing all his mysteries and making everything plain as day, and if I have faith that says to a mountain, "Jump," and it jumps, but I don't love, I'm nothing. If I give everything I own to the poor and even go to the stake to be burned as a martyr, but I don't love, I've gotten nowhere. So, no matter what I say, what I believe, and what I do, I'm bankrupt without love. Love never gives up. Love cares more for others than for self.

Love doesn't want what it doesn't have. Love doesn't strut, doesn't have a swelled head, doesn't force itself on others, isn't always "me first," doesn't fly off the handle, doesn't keep score of the sins of others, doesn't revel when others grovel, takes pleasure in the flowering of truth, puts up with anything, trusts God always, always looks for the best, never looks back, but keeps going to the end.

Love never dies. Inspired speech will be over some day; praying in tongues will end; understanding will reach its limit. We know only a portion of the truth, and what we say about God is always incomplete. But when the Complete arrives, our incompletes will be canceled.

When I was an infant at my mother's breast, I gurgled and cooed like any infant. When I grew up, I left those infant ways for good. We don't yet see things clearly. We're squinting in a fog, peering through a mist. But it won't be long before the weather clears and the sun shines bright! We'll see it all then, see it all as clearly as God sees us, knowing him directly just as he knows us! But for right now, until that completeness, we have three things to do to lead us toward that consummation: Trust steadily in God, hope unswervingly, love extravagantly. And the best of the three is love.

I CORINTHIANS 13 MSG

YOU WILL KNOW THEM BY THEIR FRUIT

When the Holy Spirit controls our lives, he will produce this kind of fruit in us: love, joy, peace, patience, kindness, goodness, faithfulness, gentleness, and self-control. Here there is no conflict with the law. Those who belong to Christ Jesus have nailed the passions and desires of their sinful nature to his cross and crucified them there. If we are living now by the Holy Spirit, let us follow the Holy Spirit's leading in every part of our lives.

GALATIANS 5:22–25 NLT

THE ARMOR
OF GOD

Be strong with the Lord's mighty power. Put on all of God's armor so that you will be able to stand firm against all strategies and tricks of the Devil. For we are not fighting against people made of flesh and blood, but against the evil rulers and authorities of the unseen world, against those mighty powers of darkness who rule this world, and against wicked spirits in the heavenly realms. Use every piece of God's armor to resist the enemy in the time of evil, so that after the battle you will still be standing firm. Stand your ground, putting on the sturdy belt of truth and the body armor of God's righteousness. For shoes, put on the peace that comes from the Good News, so that you will be fully prepared. In every battle you will need faith as your shield to stop the fiery arrows aimed at you by Satan. Put on salvation as your helmet, and take the sword of the Spirit, which is the word of God. Pray at all times and on every occasion in the power of the Holy Spirit. Stay alert and be persistent in your prayers for all Christians everywhere.

EPHESIANS 6:10–18 NLT

INSTEAD OF WORRY, PRAY AND THINK ON THESE THINGS

Do not fret or have any anxiety about anything, but in every circumstance and in everything, by prayer and petition (definite requests), with thanksgiving, continue to make your wants known to God. And God's peace [shall be yours, that tranquil state of a soul assured of its salvation through Christ, and so fearing nothing from God and being content with its earthly lot of whatever sort that is, that peace] which transcends all understanding shall garrison and mount guard over your hearts and minds in Christ Jesus.

For the rest, brethren, whatever is true, whatever is worthy of reverence and is honorable and seemly, whatever is just, whatever is pure, whatever is lovely and lovable, whatever is kind and winsome and gracious, if there is any virtue and excellence, if there is anything worthy of praise, think on and weigh and take account of these things [fix your minds on them]. Practice what you have learned and received and heard and seen in me, and model your way of living on it, and the God of peace (of untroubled, undisturbed well-being) will be with you.

PHILIPPIANS 4:6–9 AB

FAITH IS . . .

Faith means being sure of the things we hope for and knowing that something is real even if we do not see it. Faith is the reason we remember great people who lived in the past. It is by faith we understand that the whole world was made by God's command so what we see was made by something that cannot be seen.... Without faith no one can please God. Anyone who comes to God must believe that he is real and that he rewards those who truly want to find him.

HEBREWS 11:1–3, 6 NCV

278

WALKING IN THE LIGHT

This is the message we have heard from Him and announce to you, that God is Light, and in Him there is no darkness at all. If we say that we have fellowship with Him and yet walk in the darkness, we lie and do not practice the truth; but if we walk in the Light as He Himself is in the Light, we have fellowship with one another, and the blood of Jesus His Son cleanses us from all sin. If we say that we have no sin, we are deceiving ourselves and the truth is not in us. If we confess our sins, He is faithful and righteous to forgive us our sins and to cleanse us from all unrighteousness. If we say that we have not sinned, we make Him a liar and His word is not in us.

1 JOHN 1:5–10 NASB

WORTHY IS THE LAMB

I saw in the right hand of Him who sat on the throne a scroll written inside and on the back, sealed with seven seals. Then I saw a strong angel proclaiming with a loud voice, "Who is worthy to open the scroll and to loose its seals?" And no one in heaven or on the earth or under the earth was able to open the scroll, or to look at it. So I wept much, because no one was found worthy to open and read the scroll, or to look at it. But one of the elders said to me, "Do not weep. Behold, the Lion of the tribe of Judah, the Root of David, has prevailed to open the scroll and to loose its seven seals."

And I looked, and behold, in the midst of the throne and of the four living creatures, and in the midst of the elders, stood a Lamb as though it had been slain, having seven horns and seven eyes, which are the seven Spirits of God sent out into all the earth. The He came and took the scroll out of the right hand of Him who sat on the throne. Now when He had taken the scroll, the four living creatures and the twenty-four elders fell down before the Lamb, each having a harp, and golden bowls full of incense, which are the prayers of the saints. And they sang a new song, saying, "You are worthy to take the scroll, and to open its seals; for You were slain, and have redeemed us to God by Your blood out of every tribe and tongue and people and nation, and have made us kings and priests to our God; and we shall reign on the earth."

REVELATION 5:1–10 NKJV

A NEW HEAVEN AND A NEW EARTH

Now I saw a new heaven and a new earth, for the first heaven and the first earth had passed away. Also there was no more sea. Then I, John, saw the holy city, New Jerusalem, coming down out of heaven from God, prepared as a bride adorned for her husband. And I heard a loud voice from heaven saying, "Behold, the tabernacle of God is with men, and He will dwell with them, and they shall be His people. God Himself will be with them and be their God. And God will wipe away every tear from their eyes; there shall be no more death, nor sorrow, nor crying. There shall be no more pain, for the former things have passed away."

REVELATION 21:1–4 NKJV

A loving Personality dominates the Bible, walking among the trees of the garden and breathing fragrance over every scene. Always a living Person is present, speaking, pleading, loving, working, and manifesting himself whenever and wherever his people have the receptivity necessary to receive the manifestation.

—A. W. TOZER

STORIES OF GREAT CHALLENGE IN THE BIBLE

EVERY CALLING IS GREAT WHEN GREATLY PURSUED.

—OLIVER WENDELL HOLMES

MY BROTHERS, BE ALL THE MORE EAGER TO MAKE YOUR CALLING AND ELECTION SURE. FOR IF YOU DO THESE THINGS, YOU WILL NEVER FALL, AND YOU WILL RECEIVE A RICH WELCOME INTO THE ETERNAL KINGDOM OF OUR LORD AND SAVIOR JESUS CHRIST.

—2 PETER 1:10-11

David

The LORD said to Samuel, "How long will you grieve over Saul? I have rejected him from being king over Israel. Fill your horn with oil and set out; I will send you to Jesse the Bethlehemite, for I have provided for myself a king among his sons."

Samuel said, "How can I go? If Saul hears of it, he will kill me." And the LORD said, "Take a heifer with you, and say, 'I have come to sacrifice to the LORD.' Invite Jesse to the sacrifice, and I will show you what you shall do; and you shall anoint for me the one whom I name to you." Samuel did what the LORD commanded, and came to Bethlehem. The elders of the city came to meet him trembling, and said, "Do you come peaceably?" He said, "Peaceably; I have come to sacrifice to the LORD; sanctify yourselves and come with me to the sacrifice." And he sanctified Jesse and his sons and invited them to the sacrifice.

When they came, he looked on Eliab and thought, "Surely the LORD's anointed is now before the LORD." But the LORD said to Samuel, "Do not look on his appearance or on the height of his stature, because I have rejected him; for the LORD does not see as mortals see; they look on the outward appearance, but the LORD looks on the heart."

Then Jesse called Abinadab, and made him pass before Samuel. He said, "Neither has the LORD chosen this one." Then Jesse made Shammah pass by. And he said, "Neither has the LORD chosen this one." Jesse made seven of his sons pass before Samuel, and Samuel said to Jesse, "The LORD has not chosen any of these." Samuel said to Jesse, "Are all your sons here?" And he said, "There remains yet the youngest, but he is keeping the sheep." And Samuel said to Jesse, "Send and bring him; for we will not sit down until he comes here." He sent and brought him in. Now he was ruddy, and had beautiful eyes, and was handsome. The LORD said, "Rise and anoint him; for this is the one." Then Samuel took the horn of oil, and anointed him in the presence of his brothers; and the spirit of the LORD came mightily upon David from that day forward. Samuel then set out and went to Ramah.

I SAMUEL 16:1–13 NRSV

STORIES OF GREAT CHALLENGE
IN THE BIBLE

Gideon

The angel of the LORD appeared to Gideon and said, "The LORD is with you, mighty warrior!" Then Gideon said, "Sir, if the LORD is with us, why are we having so much trouble? Where are the miracles our ancestors told us he did when the LORD brought them out of Egypt? But now he has left us and has handed us over to the Midianites." The LORD turned to Gideon and said, "Go with your strength and save Israel from the Midianites. I am the one who is sending you." But Gideon answered, "Lord, how can I save Israel? My family group is the weakest in Manasseh, and I am the least important member of my family." The LORD answered him, "I will be with you. It will seem as if the Midianites you are fighting are only one man." ... Then Gideon understood he had been talking to the angel of the LORD. So Gideon cried out, "Lord GOD! I have seen the angel of the LORD face to face!" But the Lord said to Gideon, "Calm down! Don't be afraid! You will not die!" So Gideon built an altar there to worship the LORD and named it The LORD Is Peace.

JUDGES 6:12–16, 22–24 NCV

IN THE BIBLE

The Calling and Commission of Jeremiah

Now the word of the LORD came to me saying, "Before I formed you in the womb I knew you, and before you were born I consecrated you; I have appointed you a prophet to the nations." Then I said, "Alas, Lord GOD! Behold, I do not know how to speak, because I am a youth." But the LORD said to me, "Do not say, 'I am a youth,' because everywhere I send you, you shall go, and all that I command you, you shall speak. Do not be afraid of them, for I am with you to deliver you," declares the LORD. Then the LORD stretched out His hand and touched my mouth, and the LORD said to me, "Behold, I have put My words in your mouth. See, I have appointed you this day over the nations and over the kingdoms, to pluck up and to break down, to destroy and to overthrow, to build and to plant."

JEREMIAH 1:4–10 NASB

STORIES OF GREAT CHALLENGE
IN THE BIBLE

Jesus' Coming Foretold

For to us a child is born, to us a son is given, and the government will be on his shoulders. And he will be called Wonderful Counselor, Mighty God, Everlasting Father, Prince of Peace. Of the increase of his government and peace there will be no end. He will reign on David's throne and over his kingdom, establishing and upholding it with justice and righteousness from that time on and forever.

ISAIAH 9:6–7

The Commissioning of Jesus

When He had been baptized, Jesus came up immediately from the water, and behold, the heavens were opened to Him, and He saw the Spirit of God descending like a dove and alighting upon Him. And suddenly a voice came from heaven, saying, "This is My beloved Son, in whom I am well pleased."

MATTHEW 3:16–17 NKJV

IN THE BIBLE

Jesus Wrestles with His Call

Then Jesus went with his followers to a place called Gethsemane. He said to them, "Sit here while I go over there and pray." He took Peter and the two sons of Zebedee with him, and he began to be very sad and troubled. He said to them, "My heart is full of sorrow, to the point of death. Stay here and watch with me." After walking a little farther away from them, Jesus fell to the ground and prayed, "My Father, if it is possible, do not give me this cup of suffering. But do what you want, not what I want." … Then Jesus went away a second time and prayed, "My Father, if it is not possible for this painful thing to be taken from me, and if I must do it, I pray that what you want will be done." Then he went back to his followers, and again he found them asleep, because their eyes were heavy. So Jesus left them and went away and prayed a third time, saying the same thing.

MATTHEW 26:36–39, 42–44 NCV

IN THE BIBLE

Jesus Completes His Mission

Then Pilate laid open Jesus' back with a leaded whip, and the soldiers made a crown of thorns and placed it on his head and robed him in royal purple. "Hail, King of the Jews!" they mocked, and struck him with their fists.... And Pilate said to the Jews, "Here is your king!" "Away with him," they yelled. "Away with him—crucify him!" ... Then Pilate gave Jesus to them to be crucified. So they had him at last, and he was taken out of the city, carrying his cross to the place known as "The Skull," in Hebrew, "Golgotha." There they crucified him.... And Pilate posted a sign over him reading, "Jesus of Nazareth, the King of the Jews." ... Jesus knew that everything was now finished, and to fulfill the Scriptures said, "I'm thirsty." A jar of sour wine was sitting there, so a sponge was soaked in it and put on a hyssop branch and held up to his lips. When Jesus had tasted it, he said, "It is finished," and bowed his head and dismissed his spirit.

JOHN 19:1–3, 14–19, 28–30 KJV

… Jesus himself was suddenly standing there among them. He said, "Peace be with you…. Yes, it was written long ago that the Messiah must suffer and die and rise again from the dead on the third day. With my authority, take this message of repentance to all the nations, beginning in Jerusalem: 'There is forgiveness of sins for all who turn to me.'"

LUKE 24:36, 46–47 NLT

IN THE BIBLE

John the Baptist's Coming Foretold

Zacharias was in the sanctuary when suddenly an angel appeared, standing to the right of the altar of incense! Zacharias was startled and terrified. But the angel said, "Don't be afraid, Zacharias! For I have come to tell you that God has heard your prayer, and your wife Elizabeth will bear you a son! And you are to name him John. You will both have great joy and gladness at his birth, and many will rejoice with you. For he will be one of the Lord's great men. He must never touch wine or hard liquor—and he will be filled with the Holy Spirit, even from before his birth! And he will persuade many a Jew to turn to the Lord his God. He will be a man of rugged spirit and power like Elijah, the prophet of old; and he will precede the coming of the Messiah, preparing the people for his arrival. He will soften adult hearts to become like little children's, and will change disobedient minds to the wisdom of faith."

By now Elizabeth's waiting was over, for the time had come for the baby to be born—and it was a boy. Then his father,

Zacharias, was filled with the Holy Spirit and gave this prophecy: ... "And you, my little son, shall be called the prophet of the glorious God, for you will prepare the way for the Messiah. You will tell his people how to find salvation through forgiveness of their sins. All this will be because the mercy of our God is very tender, and heaven's dawn is about to break upon us, to give light to those who sit in darkness and death's shadow, and to guide us to the path of peace." The little boy greatly loved God and when he grew up he lived out in the lonely wilderness until he began his public ministry to Israel.

LUKE 1:11–17, 57, 67, 76–80 TLB

293

IN THE BIBLE

The Ministry of John the Baptist

About that time John the Baptist began preaching in the desert area of Judea. John said, "Change your hearts and lives because the kingdom of heaven is near." John the Baptist is the one Isaiah the prophet was talking about when he said, "This is a voice of one who calls out in the desert: 'Prepare the way for the Lord. Make the road straight for him.'" John's clothes were made from camel's hair, and he wore a leather belt around his waist. For food, he ate locusts and wild honey. Many people came from Jerusalem and Judea and all the area around the Jordan River to hear John. They confessed their sins, and he baptized them in the Jordan River.

MATTHEW 3:1–6 NCV

IN THE BIBLE

Mary

In the sixth month of Elizabeth's pregnancy, God sent the angel Gabriel to Nazareth, a village in Galilee, to a virgin named Mary. She was engaged to be married to a man named Joseph, a descendant of King David. Gabriel appeared to her and said, "Greetings, favored woman! The Lord is with you!" Confused and disturbed, Mary tried to think what the angel could mean. "Don't be frightened, Mary," the angel told her, "for God has decided to bless you! You will become pregnant and have a son, and you are to name him Jesus. He will be very great and will be called the Son of the Most High. And the Lord God will give him the throne of his ancestor David. And he will reign over Israel forever; his Kingdom will never end!" Mary asked the angel, "But how can I have a baby? I am a virgin." The angel replied, "The Holy Spirit will come upon you, and the power of the Most High will overshadow you. So the baby born to you will be holy, and he will be called the Son of God.... For nothing is impossible with God." Mary responded, "I am the Lord's servant, and I am willing to accept whatever he wants. May everything you have said come true." And then the angel left.

LUKE 1:26–35, 37–38 NLT

295

STORIES OF GREAT CHALLENGE
IN THE BIBLE

Moses

One day Moses was taking care of Jethro's flock.... He came to Sinai, the mountain of God. There the angel of the LORD appeared to him in flames of fire coming out of a bush. Moses saw that the bush was on fire, but it was not burning up. So he said, "I will go closer to this strange thing. How can a bush continue burning without burning up?" When the LORD saw Moses was coming to look at the bush, God called to him from the bush, "Moses, Moses!" And Moses said, "Here I am." ... The LORD said, ... "I have heard the cries of the people of Israel, and I have seen the way the Egyptians have made life hard for them. So now I am sending you to the king of Egypt. Go! Bring my people, the Israelites, out of Egypt!" But Moses said to God, "I am not a great man! How can I go to the king and lead the Israelites out of Egypt?" God said, "I will be with you. This will be the proof that I am sending you: After you lead the people out of Egypt, all of you will worship me on this mountain."

Moses said to God, "When I go to the Israelites, I will say to them, 'The God of your fathers sent me to you.' What if the people say, 'What is his name?' What should I tell them?" Then God said to Moses, "I AM WHO I AM. When you go to the people of Israel, tell them, 'I AM sent me to you.'" … Then Moses answered, "What if the people of Israel do not believe me or listen to me? What if they say, 'The LORD did not appear to you'?" The LORD said to him, "What is that in your hand?" Moses answered, "It is my walking stick." The LORD said, "Throw it on the ground." So Moses threw it on the ground, and it became a snake. Moses ran from the snake, but the LORD said to him, "Reach out and grab the snake by its tail." When Moses reached out and took hold of the snake, it again became a stick in his hand. The LORD said, "This is so that the Israelites will believe that the LORD appeared to you. I am the God of their ancestors, the God of Abraham, the God of Isaac, and the God of Jacob."

But Moses said to the LORD, "Please, LORD, I have never been a skilled speaker. Even now, after talking to you, I cannot speak well. I speak slowly and can't find the best words." Then the LORD said to him, "Who made a person's mouth? … It is I, the LORD. Now go! I will help you speak, and I will teach you what to say." But Moses said, "Please, Lord, send someone else." The LORD became angry with Moses and said, "Your brother Aaron, from the family of Levi, is a skilled speaker … You will speak to Aaron and tell him what to say. I will help both of you to speak and will teach you what to do. Aaron will speak to the people for you. You will tell him what God says, and he will speak for you. Take your walking stick with you, and use it to do the miracles." … So Moses took his wife and his sons, put them on a donkey, and started back to Egypt. He took with him the walking stick of God.

EXODUS 3:1–4, 7, 9–14; 4:1–5, 10–17, 20 NCV

IN THE BIBLE

Paul

Saul was still breathing out murderous threats against the Lord's disciples.... As he neared Damascus on his journey, suddenly a light from heaven flashed around him. He fell to the ground and heard a voice say to him, "Saul, Saul, why do you persecute me?" "Who are you, Lord?" Saul asked. "I am Jesus, whom you are persecuting," he replied. "Now get up and go into the city, and you will be told what you must do." ... In Damascus there was a disciple named Ananias. The Lord called to him in a vision, "Ananias!" "Yes, Lord," he answered. The Lord told him, "Go to the house of Judas on Straight Street and ask for a man from Tarsus named Saul, for he is praying. In a vision he has seen a man named Ananias come and place his hands on him to restore his sight." "Lord," Ananias answered, "I have heard many reports about this man and all the harm he has done to your saints in Jerusalem. And he has come here with authority from the chief priests to arrest all who call on your name."

But the Lord said to Ananias, "Go! This man is my chosen instrument to carry my name before the Gentiles and their kings and before the people of Israel. I will show him how much he must suffer for my name." Then Ananias went to the house and entered it. Placing his hands on Saul, he said, "Brother Saul, the Lord—Jesus, who appeared to you on the road as you were coming here—has sent me so that you may see again and be filled with the Holy Spirit." Immediately, something like scales fell from Saul's eyes, and he could see again. He got up and was baptized, and after taking some food, he regained his strength. Saul spent several days with the disciples in Damascus. At once he began to preach in the synagogues that Jesus is the Son of God.

ACTS 9:1, 3–6, 10–20

PRAYERS OF THE BIBLE
FOR GRADUATES

MAKE ME WHAT THOU WOULDST HAVE ME; I BARGAIN FOR
NOTHING; I MAKE NO TERMS; I SEEK FOR NO PREVIOUS
INFORMATION WHITHER THOU ART TAKING ME; I WILL BE
WHAT THOU WILT MAKE ME, AND ALL THAT THOU WILT MAKE
ME. I SAY NOT, I WILL FOLLOW THEE WHITHERSOEVER THOU
GOEST, FOR I AM WEAK; BUT I GIVE MYSELF TO
THEE TO LEAD ME ANYWHERE.

—CARDINAL JOHN HENRY NEWMAN

THE LORD BLESS YOU AND KEEP YOU; THE LORD MAKE HIS
FACE SHINE UPON YOU AND BE GRACIOUS TO YOU; THE LORD
TURN HIS FACE TOWARD YOU AND GIVE YOU PEACE.

—NUMBERS 6:24-26

FOR GRADUATES

Jesus

Jesus spoke these things; and lifting up His eyes to heaven, He said, "Father, the hour has come; glorify Your Son, that the Son may glorify You, even as You gave Him authority over all flesh, that to all whom You have given Him, He may give eternal life. This is eternal life, that they may know You, the only true God, and Jesus Christ whom You have sent. I glorified You on the earth, having accomplished the work which You have given Me to do. Now, Father, glorify Me together with Yourself, with the glory which I had with You before the world was. I have manifested Your name to the men whom You gave Me out of the world; they were Yours and You gave them to Me, and they have kept Your word. Now they have come to know that everything You have given Me is from You; for the words which You gave Me I have given to them; and they received them and truly understood that I came forth from You, and they believed that You sent Me. I ask on their behalf; I do not ask on behalf of the world, but of those whom You have given Me; for they are Yours; and all things that are Mine are Yours, and Yours are Mine; and I have been glorified in them. I am no longer in the world; and yet they themselves are in the world, and I come to You. Holy Father, keep them in Your name, the name which You have given Me, that they may be one even as We are. While I was with them, I was keeping them in Your name which You have given Me; and I guarded them and not one of them perished but the son of perdition, so that the Scripture would be fulfilled.

"But now I come to You; and these things I speak in the world so that they may have My joy made full in themselves. I have given them Your word; and the world has hated them, because they are not of the world, even as I am not of the world. I do not ask You to take them out of the world, but to keep them from the evil one. They are not of the world, even as I am not of the world. Sanctify them in the truth; Your word is truth. As You sent me into the world, I also have sent them into the world. For their sakes I sanctify Myself, that they themselves also may be sanctified in truth.

"I do not ask on behalf of these alone, but for those also who believe in Me through their word; that they may all be one; even as You, Father, are in Me and I in You, that they also may be in Us, so that the world may believe that You sent Me.

The glory which You have given Me I have given to them, that they may be one, just as We are one; I in them and You in Me, that they may be perfected in unity, so that the world may know that You sent Me, and loved them, even as You have loved Me. Father, I desire that they also, whom You have given Me, be with Me where I am, so that they may see My glory which You have given Me, for You loved Me before the foundation of the world. O righteous Father, although the world has not known You, yet I have known You; and these have known that You sent Me; and I have made Your name known to them, and will make it known, so that the love with which You loved Me may be in them, and I in them."

JOHN 17:1–26 NASB

PRAYERS OF THE BIBLE
FOR GRADUATES

Paul

I also after I heard of your faith in the Lord Jesus and your love for all the saints, do not cease to give thanks for you, making mention of you in my prayers: that the God of our Lord Jesus Christ, the Father of glory, may give to you the spirit of wisdom and revelation in the knowledge of Him, the eyes of your understanding being enlightened; that you may know what is the hope of His calling, what are the riches of the glory of His inheritance in the saints, and what is the exceeding greatness of His power toward us who believe, according to the working of His mighty power which He worked in Christ when He raised Him from the dead and seated Him at His right hand in the heavenly places.

EPHESIANS 1:15–20 NKJV

For this reason I bow my knees to the Father of our Lord Jesus Christ, from whom the whole family in heaven and earth is named, that He would grant you, according to the riches of His glory, to be strengthened with might through His Spirit in the inner man, that Christ may dwell in your hearts through faith; that you, being rooted and grounded in

305

love, may be able to comprehend with all the saints what is the width and length and depth and height—to know the love of Christ which passes knowledge; that you may be filled with all the fullness of God.

Now to Him who is able to do exceedingly abundantly above all that we ask or think, according to the power that works in us, to Him be glory in the church by Christ Jesus to all generations, forever and ever. Amen.

EPHESIANS 3:14–21 NKJV

For this reason, since the day we heard about you, we have not stopped praying for you and asking God to fill you with the knowledge of his will through all spiritual wisdom and understanding. And we pray this in order that you may live a life worthy of the Lord and may please him in every way: bearing fruit in every good work, growing in the knowledge of God, being strengthened with all power according to his glorious might so that you may have great endurance and patience, and joyfully giving thanks to the Father, who has qualified you to share in the inheritance of the saints in the kingdom of light.

COLOSSIANS 1:9–12

THROUGH THE BIBLE
IN ONE YEAR

A KNOWLEDGE OF THE BIBLE WITHOUT A COLLEGE COURSE
IS MORE VALUABLE THAN A COLLEGE COURSE
WITHOUT THE BIBLE.

—WILLIAM LYON PHELPS

THERE'S NOTHING LIKE THE WRITTEN WORD OF GOD FOR
SHOWING YOU THE WAY TO SALVATION THROUGH FAITH IN
CHRIST JESUS. EVERY PART OF SCRIPTURE IS GOD-BREATHED
AND USEFUL ONE WAY OR ANOTHER—SHOWING US TRUTH,
EXPOSING OUR REBELLION, CORRECTING OUR MISTAKES,
TRAINING US TO LIVE GOD'S WAY. THROUGH THE WORD WE
ARE PUT TOGETHER AND SHAPED UP FOR THE TASKS GOD HAS
FOR US.

—2 TIMOTHY 3:15-17 MSG

January

1. Genesis 1—2; Psalm 1; Matthew 1—2
2. Genesis 3—4; Psalm 2; Matthew 3—4
3. Genesis 5—7; Psalm 3, Matthew 5
4. Genesis 8—9; Psalm 4; Matthew 6—7
5. Genesis 10—11; Psalm 5; Matthew 8—9
6. Genesis 12—13; Psalm 6; Matthew 10—11
7. Genesis 14—15; Psalm 7; Matthew 12
8. Genesis 16—17; Psalm 8; Matthew 13
9. Genesis 18—19; Psalm 9; Matthew 14—15
10. Genesis 20—21; Psalm 10; Matthew 16—17
11. Genesis 22—23; Psalm 11; Matthew 18
12. Genesis 24; Psalm 12; Matthew 19—20
13. Genesis 25—26; Psalm 13; Matthew 21
14. Genesis 27—28; Psalm 14; Matthew 22
15. Genesis 29—30; Psalm 15; Matthew 23
16. Genesis 31—32; Psalm 16; Matthew 24
17. Genesis 33—34; Psalm 17; Matthew 25
18. Genesis 35—36; Psalm 18; Matthew 26
19. Genesis 37—38; Psalm 19; Matthew 27
20. Genesis 39—40; Psalm 20; Matthew 28
21. Genesis 41—42; Psalm 21; Mark 1
22. Genesis 43—44; Psalm 22; Mark 2
23. Genesis 45—46; Psalm 23; Mark 3
24. Genesis 47—48; Psalm 24; Mark 4
25. Genesis 49—50; Psalm 25; Mark 5
26. Exodus 1—2; Psalm 26; Mark 6
27. Exodus 3—4; Psalm 27; Mark 7
28. Exodus 5—6; Psalm 28; Mark 8
29. Exodus 7—8; Psalm 29; Mark 9
30. Exodus 9—10; Psalm 30; Mark 10
31. Exodus 11—12; Psalm 31; Mark 11

February

1. Exodus 13—14; Psalm 32; Mark 12
2. Exodus 15—16; Psalm 33; Mark 13
3. Exodus 17—18; Psalm 34; Mark 14
4. Exodus 19—20; Psalm 35; Mark 15
5. Exodus 21—22; Psalm 36; Mark 16
6. Exodus 23—24; Psalm 37; Luke 1
7. Exodus 25—26; Psalm 38; Luke 2
8. Exodus 27—28; Psalm 39; Luke 3
9. Exodus 29—30; Psalm 40; Luke 4
10. Exodus 31—32; Psalm 41; Luke 5
11. Exodus 33—34; Psalm 42; Luke 6
12. Exodus 35—36; Psalm 43; Luke 7
13. Exodus 37—38; Psalm 44; Luke 8
14. Exodus 39—40; Psalm 45; Luke 9
15. Leviticus 1—2; Psalm 46; Luke 10
16. Leviticus 3—4; Psalm 47; Luke 11
17. Leviticus 5—6; Psalm 48; Luke 12
18. Leviticus 7—8; Psalm 49; Luke 13
19. Leviticus 9—10; Psalm 50; Luke 14
20. Leviticus 11—12; Psalm 51; Luke 15
21. Leviticus 13; Psalm 52; Luke 16
22. Leviticus 14; Psalm 53; Luke 17
23. Leviticus 15—16; Psalm 54; Luke 18
24. Leviticus 17—18; Psalm 55; Luke 19
25. Leviticus 19—20; Psalm 56; Luke 20
26. Leviticus 21—22; Psalm 57; Luke 21
27. Leviticus 23—24; Psalm 58; Luke 22
28. Leviticus 25; Psalm 59; Luke 23

March

1. Leviticus 26—27; Psalm 60; Luke 24
2. Numbers 1—2; Psalm 61; John 1
3. Numbers 3—4; Psalm 62; John 2—3
4. Numbers 5—6; Psalm 63; John 4
5. Numbers 7; Psalm 64; John 5
6. Numbers 8—9; Psalm 65; John 6
7. Numbers 10—11; Psalm 66; John 7
8. Numbers 12—13; Psalm 67; John 8
9. Numbers 14—15; Psalm 68; John 9
10. Numbers 16; Psalm 69; John 10
11. Numbers 17—18; Psalm 70; John 11
12. Numbers 19—20; Psalm 71; John 12
13. Numbers 21—22; Psalm 72; John 13
14. Numbers 23—24; Psalm 73; John 14—15
15. Numbers 25—26; Psalm 74; John 16
16. Numbers 27—28; Psalm 75; John 17
17. Numbers 29—30; Psalm 76; John 18
18. Numbers 31—32; Psalm 77; John 19
19. Numbers 33—34; Psalm 78; John 20
20. Numbers 35—36; Psalm 79; John 21
21. Deuteronomy 1—2; Psalm 80; Acts 1
22. Deuteronomy 3—4; Psalm 81; Acts 2
23. Deuteronomy 5—6; Psalm 82; Acts 3—4
24. Deuteronomy 7—8; Psalm 83; Acts 5—6
25. Deuteronomy 9—10; Psalm 84; Acts 7
26. Deuteronomy 11—12; Psalm 85; Acts 8
27. Deuteronomy 13—14; Psalm 86; Acts 9
28. Deuteronomy 15—16; Psalm 87; Acts 10
29. Deuteronomy 17—18; Psalm 88; Acts 11—12
30. Deuteronomy 19—20; Psalm 89; Acts 13
31. Deuteronomy 21—22; Psalm 90; Acts 14

April

1. Deuteronomy 23—24; Psalm 91; Acts 15
2. Deuteronomy 25—27; Psalm 92; Acts 16
3. Deuteronomy 28—29; Psalm 93; Acts 17
4. Deuteronomy 30—31; Psalm 94; Acts 18
5. Deuteronomy 32; Psalm 95; Acts 19
6. Deuteronomy 33—34; Psalm 96; Acts 20
7. Joshua 1—2; Psalm 97; Acts 21
8. Joshua 3—4; Psalm 98; Acts 22
9. Joshua 5—6; Psalm 99; Acts 23
10. Joshua 7—8; Psalm 100; Acts 24—25
11. Joshua 9—10; Psalm 101; Acts 26
12. Joshua 11—12; Psalm 102; Acts 27
13. Joshua 13—14; Psalm 103; Acts 28
14. Joshua 15—16; Psalm 104; Romans 1—2
15. Joshua 17—18; Psalm 105; Romans 3—4
16. Joshua 19—20; Psalm 106; Romans 5—6
17. Joshua 21—22; Psalm 107; Romans 7—8
18. Joshua 23—24; Psalm 108; Romans 9—10
19. Judges 1—2; Psalm 109; Romans 11—12
20. Judges 3—4; Psalm 110; Romans 13—14
21. Judges 5—6; Psalm 111; Romans 15—16
22. Judges 7—8; Psalm 112; 1 Corinthians 1—2
23. Judges 9; Psalm 113; 1 Corinthians 3—4
24. Judges 10—11; Psalm 114; 1 Corinthians 5—6
25. Judges 12—13; Psalm 115; 1 Corinthians 7
26. Judges 14—15; Psalm 116; 1 Corinthians 8—9
27. Judges 16—17; Psalm 117; 1 Corinthians 10
28. Judges 18—19; Psalm 118; 1 Corinthians 11
29. Judges 20—21; Psalm 119:1–88; 1 Corinthians 12
30. Ruth 1—4; Psalm 119:89–176; 1 Corinthians 13

May

1. 1 Samuel 1—2; Psalm 120; 1 Corinthians 14
2. 1 Samuel 3—4; Psalm 121; 1 Corinthians 15
3. 1 Samuel 5—6; Psalm 122; 1 Corinthians 16
4. 1 Samuel 7—8; Psalm 123; 2 Corinthians 1
5. 1 Samuel 9—10; Psalm 124; 2 Corinthians 2—3
6. 1 Samuel 11—12; Psalm 125; 2 Corinthians 4—5
7. 1 Samuel 13—14; Psalm 126; 2 Corinthians 6—7
8. 1 Samuel 15—16; Psalm 127; 2 Corinthians 8
9. 1 Samuel 17; Psalm 128; 2 Corinthians 9—10
10. 1 Samuel 18—19; Psalm 129; 2 Corinthians 11
11. 1 Samuel 20—21; Psalm 130; 2 Corinthians 12
12. 1 Samuel 22—23; Psalm 131; 2 Corinthians 13
13. 1 Samuel 24—25; Psalm 132; Galatians 1—2
14. 1 Samuel 26—27; Psalm 133; Galatians 3—4
15. 1 Samuel 28—29; Psalm 134; Galatians 5—6
16. 1 Samuel 30—31; Psalm 135; Ephesians 1—2
17. 2 Samuel 1—2; Psalm 136; Ephesians 3—4
18. 2 Samuel 3—4; Psalm 137; Ephesians 5—6
19. 2 Samuel 5—6; Psalm 138; Philippians 1—2
20. 2 Samuel 7—8; Psalm 139; Philippians 3—4
21. 2 Samuel 9—10; Psalm 140; Colossians 1—2
22. 2 Samuel 11—12; Psalm 141; Colossians 3—4
23. 2 Samuel 13—14; Psalm 142; 1 Thessalonians 1—2
24. 2 Samuel 15—16; Psalm 143; 1 Thessalonians 3—4
25. 2 Samuel 17—18; Psalm 144; 1 Thessalonians 5
26. 2 Samuel 19; Psalm 145; 2 Thessalonians 1—3
27. 2 Samuel 20—21; Psalm 146; 1 Timothy 1—2
28. 2 Samuel 22; Psalm 147; 1 Timothy 3—4
29. 2 Samuel 23—24; Psalm 148; 1 Timothy 5—6
30. 1 Kings 1; Psalm 149; 2 Timothy 1—2
31. 1 Kings 2—3; Psalm 150; 2 Timothy 3—4

June

1. 1 Kings 4—5; Proverbs 1; Titus 1—3
2. 1 Kings 6—7; Proverbs 2; Philemon
3. 1 Kings 8; Proverbs 3; Hebrews 1—2
4. 1 Kings 9—10; Proverbs 4; Hebrews 3—4
5. 1 Kings 11—12; Proverbs 5; Hebrews 5—6
6. 1 Kings 13—14; Proverbs 6; Hebrews 7—8
7. 1 Kings 15—16; Proverbs 7; Hebrews 9—10
8. 1 Kings 17—18; Proverbs 8; Hebrews 11
9. 1 Kings 19—20; Proverbs 9; Hebrews 12
10. 1 Kings 21—22; Proverbs 10; Hebrews 13
11. 2 Kings 1—2; Proverbs 11; James 1
12. 2 Kings 3—4; Proverbs 12; James 2—3
13. 2 Kings 5—6; Proverbs 13; James 4—5
14. 2 Kings 7—8; Proverbs 14; 1 Peter 1
15. 2 Kings 9—10; Proverbs 15; 1 Peter 2—3
16. 2 Kings 11—12; Proverbs 16; 1 Peter 4—5
17. 2 Kings 13—14; Proverbs 17; 2 Peter 1—3
18. 2 Kings 15—16; Proverbs 18; 1 John 1—2
19. 2 Kings 17; Proverbs 19; 1 John 3—4
20. 2 Kings 18—19; Proverbs 20; 1 John 5
21. 2 Kings 20—21; Proverbs 21; 2 John
22. 2 Kings 22—23; Proverbs 22; 3 John
23. 2 Kings 24—25; Proverbs 23; Jude
24. 1 Chronicles 1; Proverbs 24; Revelation 1—2
25. 1 Chronicles 2—3; Proverbs 25; Revelation 3—5
26. 1 Chronicles 4—5; Proverbs 26; Revelation 6—7
27. 1 Chronicles 6—7; Proverbs 27; Revelation 8—10
28. 1 Chronicles 8—9; Proverbs 28; Revelation 11—12
29. 1 Chronicles 10—11; Proverbs 29; Revelation 13—14
30. 1 Chronicles 12—13; Proverbs 30; Revelation 15—17

July

1. 1 Chronicles 14—15; Proverbs 31; Revelation 18—19
2. 1 Chronicles 16—17; Psalm 1; Revelation 20—22
3. 1 Chronicles 18—19; Psalm 2; Matthew 1—2
4. 1 Chronicles 20—21; Psalm 3; Matthew 3—4
5. 1 Chronicles 22—23; Psalm 4; Matthew 5
6. 1 Chronicles 24—25; Psalm 5; Matthew 6—7
7. 1 Chronicles 26—27; Psalm 6; Matthew 8—9
8. 1 Chronicles 28—29; Psalm 7; Matthew 10—11
9. 2 Chronicles 1—2; Psalm 8; Matthew 12
10. 2 Chronicles 3—4; Psalm 9; Matthew 13
11. 2 Chronicles 5—6; Psalm 10; Matthew 14—15
12. 2 Chronicles 7—8; Psalm 11; Matthew 16—17
13. 2 Chronicles 9—10; Psalm 12; Matthew 18
14. 2 Chronicles 11—12; Psalm 13; Matthew 19—20
15. 2 Chronicles 13—14; Psalm 14; Matthew 21
16. 2 Chronicles 15—16; Psalm 15; Matthew 22
17. 2 Chronicles 17—18; Psalm 16; Matthew 23
18. 2 Chronicles 19—20; Psalm 17; Matthew 24
19. 2 Chronicles 21—22; Psalm 18; Matthew 25
20. 2 Chronicles 23—24; Psalm 19; Matthew 26
21. 2 Chronicles 25—26; Psalm 20; Matthew 27
22. 2 Chronicles 27—28; Psalm 21; Matthew 28
23. 2 Chronicles 29—30; Psalm 22; Mark 1
24. 2 Chronicles 31—32; Psalm 23; Mark 2
25. 2 Chronicles 33—34; Psalm 24; Mark 3
26. 2 Chronicles 35—36; Psalm 25; Mark 4
27. Ezra 1—2; Psalm 26; Mark 5
28. Ezra 3—4; Psalm 27; Mark 6
29. Ezra 5—6; Psalm 28; Mark 7
30. Ezra 7—8; Psalm 29; Mark 8
31. Ezra 9—10; Psalm 30; Mark 9

August

1. Nehemiah 1—2; Psalm 31; Mark 10
2. Nehemiah 3—4; Psalm 32; Mark 11
3. Nehemiah 5—6; Psalm 33; Mark 12
4. Nehemiah 7; Psalm 34; Mark 13
5. Nehemiah 8—9; Psalm 35; Mark 14
6. Nehemiah 10—11; Psalm 36; Mark 15
7. Nehemiah 12—13; Psalm 37; Mark 16
8. Esther 1—2; Psalm 38; Luke 1
9. Esther 3—4; Psalm 39; Luke 2
10. Esther 5—6; Psalm 40; Luke 3
11. Esther 7—8; Psalm 41; Luke 4
12. Esther 9—10; Psalm 42; Luke 5
13. Job 1—2; Psalm 43; Luke 6
14. Job 3—4; Psalm 44; Luke 7
15. Job 5—6; Psalm 45; Luke 8
16. Job 7—8; Psalm 46; Luke 9
17. Job 9—10; Psalm 47; Luke 10
18. Job 11—12; Psalm 48; Luke 11
19. Job 13—14; Psalm 49; Luke 12
20. Job 15—16; Psalm 50; Luke 13
21. Job 17—18; Psalm 51; Luke 14
22. Job 19—20; Psalm 52; Luke 15
23. Job 21—22; Psalm 53; Luke 16
24. Job 23—25; Psalm 54; Luke 17
25. Job 26—28; Psalm 55; Luke 18
26. Job 29—30; Psalm 56; Luke 19
27. Job 31—32; Psalm 57; Luke 20
28. Job 33—34; Psalm 58; Luke 21
29. Job 35—36; Psalm 59; Luke 22
30. Job 37—38; Psalm 60; Luke 23
31. Job 39—40; Psalm 61; Luke 24

September

1. Job 41—42; Psalm 62; John 1
2. Ecclesiastes 1—2; Psalm 63; John 2—3
3. Ecclesiastes 3—4; Psalm 64; John 4
4. Ecclesiastes 5—6; Psalm 65; John 5
5. Ecclesiastes 7—8; Psalm 66; John 6
6. Ecclesiastes 9—10; Psalm 67; John 7
7. Ecclesiastes 11—12; Psalm 68; John 8
8. Song of Solomon 1—2; Psalm 69; John 9
9. Song of Solomon 3—4; Psalm 70; John 10
10. Song of Solomon 5—6; Psalm 71; John 11
11. Song of Solomon 7—8; Psalm 72; John 12
12. Isaiah 1—2; Psalm 73; John 13
13. Isaiah 3—5; Psalm 74; John 14—15
14. Isaiah 6—8; Psalm 75; John 16
15. Isaiah 9—10; Psalm 76; John 17
16. Isaiah 11—13; Psalm 77; John 18
17. Isaiah 14—15; Psalm 78; John 19
18. Isaiah 16—17; Psalm 79; John 20
19. Isaiah 18—19; Psalm 80; John 21
20. Isaiah 20—22; Psalm 81; Acts 1
21. Isaiah 23—24; Psalm 82; Acts 2
22. Isaiah 25—26; Psalm 83; Acts 3—4
23. Isaiah 27—28; Psalm 84; Acts 5—6
24. Isaiah 29—30; Psalm 85; Acts 7
25. Isaiah 31—32; Psalm 86; Acts 8
26. Isaiah 33—34; Psalm 87; Acts 9
27. Isaiah 35—36; Psalm 88; Acts 10
28. Isaiah 37—38; Psalm 89; Acts 11—12
29. Isaiah 39—40; Psalm 90; Acts 13
30. Isaiah 41—42; Psalm 91; Acts 14

October

1. Isaiah 43—44; Psalm 92; Acts 15
2. Isaiah 45—46; Psalm 93; Acts 16
3. Isaiah 47—48; Psalm 94; Acts 17
4. Isaiah 49—50; Psalm 95; Acts 18
5. Isaiah 51—52; Psalm 96; Acts 19
6. Isaiah 53—54; Psalm 97; Acts 20
7. Isaiah 55—56; Psalm 98; Acts 21
8. Isaiah 57—58; Psalm 99; Acts 22
9. Isaiah 59—60; Psalm 100; Acts 23
10. Isaiah 61—62; Psalm 101; Acts 24—25
11. Isaiah 63—64; Psalm 102; Acts 26
12. Isaiah 65—66; Psalm 103; Acts 27
13. Jeremiah 1—2; Psalm 104; Acts 28
14. Jeremiah 3—4; Psalm 105; Romans 1—2
15. Jeremiah 5—6; Psalm 106; Romans 3—4
16. Jeremiah 7—8; Psalm 107; Romans 5—6
17. Jeremiah 9—10; Psalm 108; Romans 7—8
18. Jeremiah 11—12; Psalm 109; Romans 9—10
19. Jeremiah 13—14; Psalm 110; Romans 11—12
20. Jeremiah 15—16; Psalm 111; Romans 13—14
21. Jeremiah 17—18; Psalm 112; Romans 15—16
22. Jeremiah 19—20; Psalm 113; 1 Corinthians 1—2
23. Jeremiah 21—22; Psalm 114; 1 Corinthians 3—4
24. Jeremiah 23—24; Psalm 115; 1 Corinthians 5—6
25. Jeremiah 25—26; Psalm 116; 1 Corinthians 7
26. Jeremiah 27—28; Psalm 117; 1 Corinthians 8—9
27. Jeremiah 29—30; Psalm 118; 1 Corinthians 10
28. Jeremiah 31—32; Psalm 119:1—64; 1 Corinthians 11
29. Jeremiah 33—34; Psalm 119:65—120; 1 Corinthians 12
30. Jeremiah 35—36; Psalm 119:121—176; 1 Corinthians 13
31. Jeremiah 37—38; Psalm 120; 1 Corinthians 14

November

1. Jeremiah 39—40; Psalm 121; 1 Corinthians 15
2. Jeremiah 41—42; Psalm 122; 1 Corinthians 16
3. Jeremiah 43—44; Psalm 123; 2 Corinthians 1
4. Jeremiah 45—46; Psalm 124; 2 Corinthians 2—3
5. Jeremiah 47—48; Psalm 125; 2 Corinthians 4—5
6. Jeremiah 49—50; Psalm 126; 2 Corinthians 6—7
7. Jeremiah 51—52; Psalm 127; 2 Corinthians 8
8. Lamentations 1—2; Psalm 128; 2 Corinthians 9—10
9. Lamentations 3; Psalm 129; 2 Corinthians 11
10. Lamentations 4—5; Psalm 130; 2 Corinthians 12
11. Ezekiel 1—2; Psalm 131; 2 Corinthians 13
12. Ezekiel 3—4; Psalm 132; Galatians 1—2
13. Ezekiel 5—6; Psalm 133; Galatians 3—4
14. Ezekiel 7—8; Psalm 134; Galatians 5—6
15. Ezekiel 9—10; Psalm 135; Ephesians 1—2
16. Ezekiel 11—12; Psalm 136; Ephesians 3—4
17. Ezekiel 13—14; Psalm 137; Ephesians 5—6
18. Ezekiel 15—16; Psalm 138; Philippians 1—2
19. Ezekiel 17—18; Psalm 139; Philippians 3—4
20. Ezekiel 19—20; Psalm 140; Colossians 1—2
21. Ezekiel 21—22; Psalm 141; Colossians 3—4
22. Ezekiel 23—24; Psalm 142; 1 Thessalonians 1—2
23. Ezekiel 25—26; Psalm 143; 1 Thessalonians 3—4
24. Ezekiel 27—28; Psalm 144; 1 Thessalonians 5
25. Ezekiel 29—30; Psalm 145; 2 Thessalonians 1—3
26. Ezekiel 31—32; Psalm 146; 1 Timothy 1—2
27. Ezekiel 33—34; Psalm 147; 1 Timothy 3—4
28. Ezekiel 35—36; Psalm 148; 1 Timothy 5—6
29. Ezekiel 37—38; Psalm 149; 2 Timothy 1—2
30. Ezekiel 39—40; Psalm 150; 2 Timothy 3—4

December

1. Ezekiel 41—42; Proverbs 1; Titus 1—3
2. Ezekiel 43—44; Proverbs 2; Philemon
3. Ezekiel 45—46; Proverbs 3; Hebrews 1—2
4. Ezekiel 47—48; Proverbs 4; Hebrews 3—4
5. Daniel 1—2; Proverbs 5; Hebrews 5—6
6. Daniel 3—4; Proverbs 6; Hebrews 7—8
7. Daniel 5—6; Proverbs 7; Hebrews 9—10
8. Daniel 7—8; Proverbs 8; Hebrews 11
9. Daniel 9—10; Proverbs 9; Hebrews 12
10. Daniel 11—12; Proverbs 10; Hebrews 13
11. Hosea 1—3; Proverbs 11; James 1—3
12. Hosea 4—6; Proverbs 12; James 4—5
13. Hosea 7—8; Proverbs 13; 1 Peter 1
14. Hosea 9—11; Proverbs 14; 1 Peter 2—3
15. Hosea 12—14; Proverbs 15; 1 Peter 4—5
16. Joel 1—3; Proverbs 16; 2 Peter 1—3
17. Amos 1—3; Proverbs 17; 1 John 1—2
18. Amos 4—6; Proverbs 18; 1 John 3—4
19. Amos 7—9; Proverbs 19; 1 John 5
20. Obadiah; Proverbs 20; 2 John
21. Jonah; Proverbs 21; 3 John
22. Micah 1—4; Proverbs 22; Jude
23. Micah 5—7; Proverbs 23; Revelation 1—2
24. Nahum; Proverbs 24; Revelation 3—5
25. Habakkuk; Proverbs 25; Revelation 6—7
26. Zephaniah; Proverbs 26; Revelation 8—10
27. Haggai; Proverbs 27; Revelation 11—12
28. Zechariah 1—4; Proverbs 28; Revelation 13—14
29. Zechariah 5—9; Proverbs 29; Revelation 15—17
30. Zechariah 10—14; Proverbs 30; Revelation 18—19
31. Malachi; Proverbs 31; Revelation 20—22

Additional copies of this and other Honor titles
are available wherever good books are sold.

◆

If you have enjoyed this book,
or if it has had an impact on your life,
we would like to hear from you.

Please contact us at

Honor Books
Cook Communications Ministries, Dept. 240
4050 Lee Vance View
Colorado Springs, CO 80918

Or visit our Web site
www.cookministries.com

HONOR HB BOOKS
Inspiration and Motivation for the Seasons of Life